10/12

curriculum
connections

Civil War
Behind the Fighting

BROWN
BEAR
BOOKS

Published by Brown Bear Books Ltd

4877 N. Circulo Bujia
Tucson
AZ 85718
USA

First Floor
9–17 St. Albans Place
London N1 0NX
UK

Managing Editor: Tim Cooke
Designer: Joan Curtis
Picture Researcher: Sophie Mortimer
Art Director: Jeni Child
Editorial Director: Lindsey Lowe

Library of Congress Cataloging-in-Publication Data

Behind the fighting / edited by Tim Cooke.
    p. cm. -- (Curriculum connections: Civil War)
 Includes index.
 Summary: "In an alphabetical almanac format, describes the people, attitudes, conditions, and events that were part of a soldier's life beyond the battle field before and after the fighting broke out"--Provided by publisher.
 ISBN 978-1-936333-44-8 (library binding)
1. United States--Armed Forces--Military life--History--19th century--Encyclopedias, Juvenile. 2. United States--History--Civil War, 1861-1865--Encyclopedias, Juvenile. 3. Soldiers--United States--History--19th century--Encyclopedias, Juvenile. I. Cooke, Tim, 1961- II. Title. III. Series.

E607.B435 2012
973.7--dc22

2011005395

Picture Credits

Cover Image
Robert Hunt Library

Picture Credits
Library of Congress 8, 24, 42, 44, 46, 62, 65, 70, 72, 76, 80, 87, 89, 93, 96, 101; National Archives 7, 15, 21, 26, 38, 56, 60, 98; New York Historical Society 84; Photodisc: 52; U.S. Army Quartermaster Museum: 104; www.lindapages.com: 34

Artwork © Brown Bear Books Ltd

Printed in the United States of America

Contents

Introduction

Civil War forms part of the Curriculum Connections series. Each of the six volumes of the set covers a particular aspect of the conflict: Home Front and the Economy; Behind the Fighting; Weapons, Tactics, and Strategy; Politics; Battles and Campaigns; and People.

About this set

Each volume in *Civil War* features illustrated chapters, providing in-depth information about each subject. The chapters are all listed in the contents pages of each book. Each volume can be studied to provide a comprehensive understanding of all aspects of the conflict. However, each chapter may also be studied independently.

Within each chapter there are two key aids to learning that are to be found in color sidebars located in the margins of each page:

Curriculum Context sidebars indicate to the reader that a subject has a particular relevance to certain key state and national history guidelines and curricula. They highlight essential information or suggest useful ways for students to consider a subject or to include it in their studies.

Glossary sidebars define key words within the text.

At the end of the book, a summary **Glossary** lists the key terms defined in the volume. There is also a list of further print and Web-based resources and a full volume index.

Fully captioned illustrations play an important role throughout the set, including photographs and explanatory maps.

About this book

Behind the Fighting explores aspects of how those caught up in the conflict experienced its effects. It also shows how news about events on the battlefield reached the people at home.

Many of the topics covered in this volume describe the many different ways in which soldiers were supported, from their recruitment and training to how they lived in camp, where they slept, and what they ate. There are also articles on the uniforms they wore and the music and mascots that accompanied them into battle. Battlefield medicine developed rapidly during the war, and all aspects of surgery and nursing care are described in the volume.

One of the most important wider developments of the Civil War was the public's awareness of what was happening on the frontline. People knew more about what had happened quicker than ever before thanks to technological innovations such as photography and the telegraph and to brave individuals who acted as special war correspondents and artists.

The reaction to the war was profound; its effects still echo in popular culture today. This volume explores the earliest impact of the conflict on contemporary artists and writers, as well as the emergence of national cemeteries and other means of commemorating the sacrifice of those who died.

Artists and Illustrators

Throughout the Civil War artists were dispatched to the front line to produce illustrations of the conflict for newspapers and periodicals. These men were considered reporters and referred to by their papers as "special artists."

Curriculum Context

What difference might have made by the public seeing what was happening on the battlefields?

Images of the Civil War were relayed to the American public to an extent not seen before in war. Although today the best-known images of the conflict are the photographs by Mathew Brady and others, the public at the time was more familiar with the black-and-white illustrations produced in periodicals such as *Harper's Weekly* and *Frank Leslie's Illustrated Newspaper*.

Photography was still in its infancy. Cameras did not have a fast enough shutter speed to take action shots, so images of battlefield action came from artists' sketches. In addition, many of the photographs taken remained classified until late in the 19th century. It was artists and engravers who shaped the public's view of the war as it occurred.

Classified

Declared an official secret by the government.

"Special artists" went to the battlefront as artist–reporters. A few, such as Alfred Waud, his brother William, and Edwin Forbes, gained popularity for their individual style and attracted a following. Other artists were more anonymous. Artists working for the foreign press also produced illustrations of the war, notably Frank Vizetelly, who covered the conflict from the Confederate side for the British *Illustrated London News*.

Woodblock

A form of printing that carves lines into a piece of wood to print.

The "specials" produced sketches that were made into woodblock engravings to print. The style of the artist was partly lost in this process, which turned subtle drawing into flat, blocked lines. Today the original sketches of artists such as Alfred Waud are valued for their delicacy as well as their subject matter.

Soldier artists

Many illustrations were made by soldiers themselves. Newspapers included advertisements recruiting artists who were about to enlist. Julian Scott and Charles W. Reed were among the artists who were serving Union soldiers. Scott's most famous work is *The Drummer Boy*, while Reed produced humorous illustrations for *Hardtack and Coffee*, a popular book published in 1887.

Winslow Homer

One war artist who went on to become a celebrated painter was Winslow Homer (1836–1910), who worked during the conflict as an artist for *Harper's Weekly*. Homer depicted the squalor and boredom of camp life while giving his soldiers a quiet grandeur. *Home Sweet Home* (1863) shows a soldier in camp making the most of his makeshift surroundings. In *Prisoners from the Front* (1866) a tall, arrogant Confederate cavalryman and two other prisoners stand before their Union captors. Homer expertly captures the tension between the men. His interest in the way ordinary soldiers looked and acted shaped a new genre of military art.

Interest from abroad

The most famous of the foreign artists who depicted the Civil War was the French Impressionist Edouard

Curriculum Context

Homer's war paintings could be included in a discussion of currents and themes in American art in the 19th century.

Winslow Homer's *Drum and Bugle Corps* (1865). Homer was a freelance illustrator who followed the Army of the Potomac. He was drawn to scenes of everyday soldier life rather than battle action and produced a number of oil paintings in the genre.

Alfred Waud made this pencil and white paint sketch at Gettysburg on July 3, 1863. It shows swaths of smoke hiding the Union forces just before the Confederates launched their last doomed offensive of the battle, Pickett's Charge.

Commerce raider

A fast ship used to intercept Union ships at sea and seize their cargo.

Manet (1832–1883). He painted a battle he witnessed at the French port of Cherbourg between the Confederate commerce raider CSS *Alabama* and the Union warship USS *Kearsarge*. James Walker, meanwhile, painted a notable depiction of the Battle of Lookout Mountain. The battle was a Union victory, and Walker was commissioned to do the painting by the victorious Union general, Joseph Hooker, for $20,000.

Curriculum Context

Cole was seen as the founder of the Hudson River School, a group of artists who were inspired by the landscapes of upstate New York and the western frontier.

Haunted memory

Before the Civil War American art had been dominated by the sense of wonder felt by European settlers at the sheer size and richness of the land they had occupied. The American painter Thomas Cole (1801–1848) declared that American artists had "privileges superior to any other. All nature here is new to art." Other artists reveling in America's size and beauty were Frederick Edwin Church (1826–1900) and Albert Bierstadt (1830–1902). William Sidney Mount (1807–1868) and George Caleb Bingham (1811–1879) painted outdoor scenes of everyday American life.

War brought horrors that demanded and inspired new ways of seeing; in its aftermath doubt, tension, and danger crept into depictions of the great wide-open spaces of North America.

Winslow Homer's postwar work continued to have an undercurrent of psychological tension. In *The Veteran in a New Field* (1865) he painted a Confederate soldier harvesting wheat. The empty field feels full of ghosts, a reminder that the land was recently a battleground.

Homer's near contemporaries Thomas Eakins (1844–1916) and Albert Pinkham Ryder (1848–1917) did not witness the Civil War at first hand, but they learned its artistic lessons through the older man's work. Among other noted postwar artists were the Southern veterans Allen C. Redwood, Conrad W. Chapman, and William L. Shepherd.

Striking images

Some Civil War pictures had an immediate effect on public opinion. George Caleb Bingham covered the Civil War. His *Order No. 11*—a painting of Missouri residents being driven from their homes by Union troops—provoked widespread public contempt, even in the North, for the army's conduct.

Curriculum Context

It might be interesting to compare Bingham's painting with images that affected public opinion in later wars, such as World War II and Vietnam.

Other works eroded the idea of military glory. Winslow Homer painted *The Sharpshooter* (1862) showing a lone sniper sitting in a tree, hidden from his target. Homer wrote to a friend that this "struck me as being as near murder as anything I could ever think of in connection with the army."

Close to the Battle

Artists, like reporters, photographers, and nurses, often found themselves in danger. The photographer Mathew Brady and the illustrator Alfred Waud were almost captured by the Confederates at the First Battle of Bull Run, when they found themselves too close to the action.

Alfred Waud spent much time with soldiers in camp and in battle, and shared their experiences. When his work took him onto the battlefield, Waud was usually weighed down with drawing gear, haversack, bowie knife, revolver, flask, and a bedroll.

Camp Followers

During the Civil War most army units were attended by hundreds of people, called camp followers, who followed the army for profit or employment. Many were officially recognized and encouraged by the armies of both sides.

Curriculum Context

If curricula ask students to understand soldiers' experience during the war, camp followers are an important factor to include.

Cardsharper

A gambler who cheats by manipulating playing cards.

Among the most useful camp followers were bakers, barbers, contract laborers, laundresses, private physicians, private servants, slaves, and refugee slaves (contrabands). There were also numerous traveling sellers of provisions: the men who did this were known as sutlers, the women as vivandières. The vivandières often carried out other roles as well, as mascots and nurses, and sometimes wore a stylized uniform. Such camp followers had a semiofficial status within regiments and were governed by army regulations.

There were also many other less respectable camp followers, but even they were usually tolerated. They included many prostitutes, but also black marketeers, illegal whiskey sellers (soldiers were forbidden alcohol), cardsharpers, and other criminals and tricksters.

friends and family

Many female camp followers were relatives of the soldiers. These women often did most of the cooking. They washed and sewed uniforms, and cared for the sick and wounded. A few women even took up arms and went into action.

Sutlers

Other camp followers had no such affiliations and were concerned only with making money. Sutlers were particularly notorious for their greed. They often did not care which side they sold to. Some of the most enterprising sutlers diversified into catering, selling pickles, cheese, homemade cakes, and dumplings.

Many soldiers complained that the sutlers were profiteering and giving short measure. Despite the questionable morals of their role, sutlers were viewed as a necessary evil by the Union, and the commanders of many northern units sanctioned—and indeed benefited from—their activities. The sutlers were taxed by their unit, usually a percentage of their total month's earnings. Some of the money raised in this way was used for the benefit of the regiment—to fund military bands, for example, the education of soldiers' children, or items for wounded members of the unit.

Soldiers were forbidden to spend more than one-third of their pay on sutlers' goods, and sutlers received payment directly from the regimental paymaster. While this policy helped ensure the sutlers' continued presence, it also increased the troops' resentment. The army's tolerance of sutlers lasted only for as long as the troops were on the road or in battle. When the army entered a town, many commanders banned sutlers and ordered their men to buy from local stores.

When news of the sutlers' activities reached the North, many people began to send food parcels to their relatives in the army to save them from being fleeced. Many of these packages were stolen en route, and those that did reach their intended destination took so long to arrive that the food had often gone bad by the time it was unwrapped.

Out of control

Sometimes the number of camp followers spiraled out of control. When the Union commander William T. Sherman marched from Atlanta, Georgia, to the coast, his army was followed by thousands of stragglers, including deserters from both sides and freed slaves. Although all camp followers were meant to be subject to military discipline, this often proved difficult to enforce in practice.

Profiteering

Making unreasonably high profits by selling essential goods at high prices during a time of emergency.

Curriculum Context

What advantages would there be in soldiers shopping at local stores?

Curriculum Context

It is worth remembering that most food throughout the war was poor quality, boring, and often rotten.

Camp Life

For all the weeks of the year spent on the march and fighting, there were months when the soldiers on both sides were living in camp and attending, in the words of one participant, "to the thousand commonplace duties of a soldier."

Curriculum Context

It might be interesting to contrast the excitement felt by many volunteers with their reaction to the realities of soldier life.

To many new volunteers camp life and military discipline came as unpleasant surprises. When the war broke out, recruits from towns and cities throughout the country went to war expecting it to be an adventure. Many imagined they would join a local militia company with their friends and neighbors, spend a week or two learning basic drill, march off to meet the enemy, and perhaps be home within weeks. They did not sign up to spend time learning to be soldiers. Sergeant Vairin of the 2nd Mississippi Volunteers wrote in his diary on May 1, 1861, "Made my first detail … for guard duty to which most men objected because they said they did not enlist to do guard duty but to fight Yankees—all fun and frolic."

Fatigues and drill

The "fun and frolic" soon went out of soldiering when the hard work started. Bugles called reveille (wake-up) at 5:00 A.M. From then on for up to 16 hours a day it was an unceasing round of manual work, called fatigues, and repetitive weapon and marching exercises, called drill, until "lights out" at 9:00 P.M. Many found the rigid structure of their new lives difficult. One Confederate soldier wrote in his journal in 1862: "None can imagine, who has never experienced a soldier's life, the languor of mind, tediousness of time, as we resume day after day the monotonous duties."

Drill

Drill was a highly repetitive series of marching exercises used by armies to ensure that soldiers learned to maneuver on the battlefield almost by instinct.

Songs in camp

The men needed relief from army life, and camps were alive with diversions. Music was popular, either played by regimental bands or by the men themselves. Fiddles were highly prized, and music from banjos, flutes, and guitars was also common. The latest songbooks were found in the camps. The most popular songs tended to be either stirring tunes like the Union favorite "The Battle Cry of Freedom," for which the Southerners had their own version, or ballads like "Just before the Battle Mother," which tugged the heartstrings of that sentimental age.

Ballad

A long song that tells a narrative, which is often melancholy or concerned with loss.

Letters home

Writing letters was one of the most popular uses of soldiers' free time. Many men had never been away from their families before, and keeping in contact with home was vitally important. Literacy rates were high, particularly in Union regiments. For those who could not read or write a friend could always take dictation and read for them. Some regiments are said to have posted and received up to 600 letters in one day.

Curriculum Context

The Civil War left a richer legacy of written sources than any previous war, including diaries and letters by officers and enlisted men.

Camp sports

Soldiers played games that had originally come from England such as soccer and cricket, and organized races, wrestling, and boxing matches. The cavalry naturally held horse races whenever they could. In the winter the snow provided an outlet for pent-up energy, and snowball fights often broke out. They were large-scale exchanges in which whole regiments and even brigades took part. The biggest game in camp was baseball, either played on the diamond around four bases or around two bases, which was called townball. Officers and enlisted men played side by side, and in this way baseball lost its reputation as a gentlemen's game.

Baseball

Baseball, based on English games, had become popular around New York in the 1850s; the Civil War helped to establish its national popularity.

Gambling

If there was a competitive activity going on, someone, somewhere gambled on the winner. Gambling was strictly forbidden, but it was too widespread among

Visit to a Camp

Confederate nurse Kate Cumming made the following journal entry on July 21, 1863, after visiting the 24th Alabama Regiment in camp:

"The regiment was encamped in a grove of trees; it had a few tents for the officers and commissary stores. But the only protection the men have from the inclement weather is their blankets put up on sticks about three feet high. The men were busy preparing for supper, and I did not think looked altogether pleased at my visiting them, as their attire and employment is not such as they would wish them to be.... I could not help contrasting this camp with the one I last visited. It was when the war first commenced, and our house had been emptied of furniture to put in tents, as we thought it impossible for men to do without certain things which they had been accustomed to at home. Since then they have learned a few lessons, in this respect, as we all have."

the men for officers to be able to enforce the rules. Men bet on louse races, hog races, and even on toy boat races, but the favorites were dice and card games such as poker. On payday it was not unknown for a soldier to lose months of back pay on the walk from the pay tent to his quarters.

Sleeping under canvas

During the summer months the soldiers lived in tents. At the beginning of the war the Union army issued the wall tent. It was a very stable canvas tent held down by up to a dozen guy ropes, but it was complicated and took too long a time to pitch.

Another common type of tent, the wedge, was a triangular tent that could house four men comfortably. One of the most widely used designs was the Sibley, a high cone-shaped tent that could sleep up to a dozen men. It was too large and heavy to be taken on the march, however, when armies were in the field. On campaign the Union army used the two-man pup tent. Two men each carried equal halves, which they buttoned together and pegged down at the end of a day on the move.

The Confederates were short of all resources, including tents. Most Southern soldiers on campaign improvised brushwood shelters called shebangs, often topped with half a pup tent captured from a Union soldier. Sometimes Confederate soldiers simply wrapped themselves in a blanket to get what sleep they could.

Shebang

A word that usually describes the whole of something, as in the phrase "the whole shebang."

Winter camps

In the winter active campaigning became impossible because of the snow and mud, and encampments became semipermanent. Between December and March the armies settled down and built wooden huts, often complete with chimneys and doors. The army in camp became a small town with an array of camp followers to service the soldiers' needs. They ranged from the families of the officers to laundresses and sutlers (merchants) selling luxuries such as newspapers and tobacco.

Union soldiers outside a wedge tent. The wedge slept four men comfortably, but it was heavy. The lighter, two-man pup tent was used on campaign.

Demobilization

The defeat of the Confederacy in 1865 meant that volunteers and conscripts of North and South alike could be discharged from military service. The two sides had a very different experience of demobilization and return to civilian life.

For the Union soldiers there were victory celebrations and parades. Having accepted the Confederate surrender on April 9, 1865, General Ulysses S. Grant marched the Army of the Potomac north to Washington, D.C. They were joined there on May 23 by General William T. Sherman's Army of the Tennessee.

Curriculum Context

Abraham Lincoln had been assassinated on April 14, 1865; Johnson had been inaugurated on April 15.

Grand victory parade

On May 23, in front of cheering crowds and the new U.S. president, Andrew Johnson, the Army of the Potomac marched down Pennsylvania Avenue in Washington, D.C. Sherman's men paraded down the avenue the following day. Of the great victory review Grant would recall in his memoirs, "The sight was varied and grand: nearly all day for two successive days, from the Capitol to the Treasury Building, could be seen a mass of orderly soldiers marching in column of companies. The National flag was flying from almost every house and store; the windows were filled with spectators…."

Union demobilization

Embark

To go on board a ship, train, or airplane to make a journey.

On May 29 the first regiments of the Union armies embarked on trains for their home states. Elsewhere Union troops assembled at New Orleans, Vicksburg, and Nashville for the start of the great demobilization.

It was a remarkable job of organization that pressed into service every train and riverboat available across the country, and that turned Northern cities such as New York into huge regional transit points.

One of the greatest disasters in U.S. maritime history took place in the first weeks of demobilization. The riverboat *Sultana*, traveling on the Mississippi north of Memphis with 2,000 troops on board, caught fire and sank on April 27, killing more than 1,400 men.

There were more than one million men in the Union army in May 1865. By November the figure was reduced to 200,000 and by February 1866 to barely 80,000. Eventually the number of troops was reduced to just 27,000 men scattered across the garrisons of the western frontier—an army scarcely 10,000 stronger than the old regular army of 1860.

In their home states, the regiments paraded for the last time. They handed back their regimental colors to the governor and were broken up into companies, which were sent back to the towns from which they first mustered. On their last day of service they received their final pay from the War Department, and then they went home, ordinary citizens once more.

Garrisons

Units of soldiers maintained in towns or forts in case they are required to keep order.

Veterans' Organizations

Shortly after the Civil War former soldiers began to organize veterans' associations. The first was the Military Order of the Loyal Legion of the United States (MOLLUS), founded in 1865 by Union officers. MOLLUS specialized in publishing officers' memoirs of the war.

The largest Union veterans' organization was the Grand Army of the Republic (GAR), founded in Springfield, Illinois, in 1866. It functioned as a welfare organization protecting pension rights and providing help for widows. Membership peaked at 400,000 in 1890. The organization was dissolved in 1956.

The largest Confederate veterans' organization was the United Confederate Veterans (UCV), founded in 1889. It was inspired by the work of the GAR, but never matched that organization for numbers, reaching about 160,000, only a quarter of the Southern soldiers known to have survived the war. The UCV was dissolved in 1944.

Members of the GAR and UCV came together at Gettysburg in July 1913 to celebrate the 50th anniversary of the battle. It was the biggest single reunion of Civil War veterans. More than 50,000 former soldiers came to remember their war and the fallen of both sides.

Demobilization in the South

For the defeated Southerners, in contrast, there was no formal end to military service. The Confederacy and the armies they had served no longer existed, military organization had collapsed through defeat and desertion, and even their regimental flags were taken from them by the victors—those which the soldiers did not burn or bury first to keep them out of Union hands.

The Southerners were not treated as prisoners of war, but were released under a parole that they would not fight against the United States again. Union forces provided food rations, while Grant and other Union generals gave permission for them to keep their horses, which, under Confederate regulations, the men had supplied themselves. They were then released to find their way home as best they could.

One Northern journalist described the former Confederate soldiers as "these poor homesick boys and exhausted men wandering about in threadbare uniforms, with scanty outfit of slender haversack and blanket roll hung over their shoulders, seeking the nearest route home: they have a care-worn anxious look, a played-out manner."

Choosing exile

Former Confederate soldiers' status as paroled prisoners was lifted on May 29, 1865, in an amnesty granted by President Andrew Johnson that pardoned them for taking part in the rebellion. Some men, though, did not accept defeat or surrender. A number of senior Southern figures, such as former secretary of war and general John C. Breckinridge, chose exile abroad. West of the Mississippi General Joseph Shelby took 600 men to Mexico to establish a Confederate colony. It is estimated some 10,000 Southerners chose exile after the war.

Parole

To release a prisoner on a promise that he or she will not repeat his or her offense.

Amnesty

An act by which an authority such as a government pardons a large group of individuals.

Draft Riots

The Union began drafting men aged 20 to 45 into the army in July 1863, sparking riots throughout the North. The most violent incidents were in New York City, where rioters turned on African Americans, targeting them as a cause of the war.

The Union government's National Conscription Act of March 3, 1863, was deeply unpopular with those who could not afford to hire a substitute or pay a $300 fee to avoid military service. But opposition to the draft also grew out of racial tensions in Union cities. The war's deprivations hit hard the poor working classes, in particular the Irish Catholic immigrant community.

Violence erupts

Antidraft incidents erupted across the North in 1863. The most violent episode took place from July 13 to July 16, 1863, in New York City. On July 11, New York held its first draft lottery. Public meetings on July 12 raised antidraft feeling, and the next day an angry crowd burned the city draft offices.

By the second day the crowd was made up largely of Irish immigrants. Their targets included the homes of leading Republicans, the offices of antislavery newspapers, and even department stores. The rioters soon targeted African Americans, who were blamed as a cause of the war. Rioters lynched at least 11 people (and perhaps more), burned the city's Colored Orphan Asylum, and forced hundreds of blacks to flee the city.

The Union sent 20,000 troops, some of them shipped in from Gettysburg, to quell the uprising. Soldiers killed at least 82 rioters. Two policemen and eight soldiers also died. Order was restored by July 16, and conscription in the city resumed on August 19; but bitterness between the communities in New York City remained.

Curriculum Context

Many curricula expect students to understand the many complex causes of the Northern draft riots.

Lynch

To put someone to death by the action of a mob, often by hanging, without legal authority.

Espionage and Counterespionage

Spying was rife during the Civil War. It was an easy matter for a supporter of one side to pretend to be a supporter of the other and discover and pass on useful information. Both sides had to set up intelligence networks for the first time.

In February 1861, two months before the war broke out, the new Confederate government took steps to safeguard the security of the Southern states by jailing potential enemies. President Jefferson Davis was authorized to suspend *habeas corpus* (the fundamental law that forbids arrest and imprisonment without trial) and was given the right to allow the army to impose martial law in towns in Virginia that were in danger of Union attack.

Martial law

Law administered by the military services.

The Union government did not follow the Confederate example until war broke out in April 1861. By the end of the month Washington, D.C., was on the verge of panic. The institutions of government seemed to be collapsing as members of Congress and judges resigned to go over to the Confederacy.

Government crackdown

Matters grew worse after the discovery of a Confederate plot to assassinate President Abraham Lincoln in Baltimore, Maryland, on his way to his inauguration in Washington in March 1861. The conspiracy was only uncovered by railroad detectives. The incident heightened fears that Confederate agents were everywhere in the Union.

Assassinate

To kill someone for their political beliefs or official position.

Lincoln needed to bring the situation under control quickly. There was no police service he could call on, and so on April 27 he too withdrew the right of *habeas corpus* and handed the task of internal security over to the army's provost marshal.

Such measures gave the government a huge amount of power. The rule of law was suspended. Senior officials need only sign a paper to have someone arrested. An estimated 13,000 U.S. citizens were arrested on suspicion of involvement with the Southern cause during the war. It was in this climate of fear that the spying organizations of North and South were founded.

Union spymaster

The first Union espionage service was established by Allan Pinkerton in August 1861. Pinkerton had set up a successful detective agency in Chicago in 1852 and had foiled the Baltimore assassination plot in March. He began his war service spying for his friend, Union General George B. McClellan, in Ohio. When McClellan took command of the Army of the Potomac, Pinkerton went with him to organize an Intelligence service.

Pinkerton's agents infiltrated behind enemy lines to discover Confederate troop strengths and provide information on lines of communication such as roads, railroads, telegraph lines, and canals. Pinkerton employed both men and women as agents. Several were former slaves who could move around inside Southern territory without arousing suspicion.

Curriculum Context

Some curricula ask students to consider the effects of Lincoln's administration on civil liberties.

Infiltrate

To use disguise to pass through enemy lines.

Union secret service men at Foller's House, Cumberland Landing, Virginia, in May 1862. The service was set up by Allan Pinkerton, a private detective.

"Crazy Bet" of Richmond

Elizabeth Van Lew, who organized a Union spy ring in Richmond, Virginia, was one of the most successful Civil War spies. Lew was from one of the oldest and most respectable families in Virginia. However, she was also an ardent abolitionist who wanted to see the overthrow of slavery and the Confederacy with it.

She did not hide her views and openly visited Union prisoners in Richmond's Libby Prison, taking them food and medicine. She realized she could smuggle out news and information about troop movements and defenses. To avoid suspicion, she started to behave strangely, until she became known as "Crazy Bet." People considered her Union sympathies a harmless part of her mental instability. Under this cover she was able to continue spying unhindered.

Lew established a spy ring in Richmond with the help of her mother and her black servants (she had freed all the family slaves.) She managed to get one servant, Mary Elizabeth Bowser, to work as a maid for President Jefferson Davis inside the Confederate White House itself.

"Crazy Bet" and her spy ring were never caught. They operated in Richmond until the city fell to the Union army on April 3, 1865.

However, Pinkerton's intelligence work proved to be a failure. He consistently overestimated Confederate troop strengths. This proved disastrous in the Peninsular Campaign of 1862, when McClellan, a timid commander at the best of times, received reports that the Confederates had as many as 200,000 men. In fact, his opponent, General Robert E. Lee, fielded barely 70,000 men. Still, McClellan fought on the defensive and ultimately lost the campaign.

Counterespionage

Pinkerton achieved more success in counterespionage, when he could use his talents as a detective to uncover the operations of Confederate spies. Perhaps his greatest success was the capture of the Southern agent Rose O'Neal Greenhow, in 1861.

Greenhow was a widow who moved in the highest circles of Washington society. She used her contacts to gain valuable military intelligence. She is credited with providing Confederate General Pierre G.T. Beauregard

Curriculum Context

Spies like Greenhow are good examples of women who played an influential role in the Civil War.

with information on Union troop movements that helped the Confederate victory at the First Battle of Bull Run (Manassas) in July.

In August 1861 Pinkerton posed as an army major to gain entry to Greenhow's home and arrest her, while his agents searched for evidence. She was placed under house arrest, then imprisoned in Washington. In June 1862 she was deported to the Confederacy.

When McClellan was fired in November 1862, Pinkerton returned to Chicago and his detective agency. Espionage in the Union was reorganized. A new secret service was established under Lafayette Curry Baker.

Confederate spy service

Because of its work on codes and ciphers the Confederate spy service was part of the army's signal corps, led by Colonel William Norris. His command extended to patrols watching for enemy movements on the Potomac River and to agents operating in Northern cities. It was highly effective and reliable.

House arrest

A form of imprisonment in which the inmate lives at home but is under guard and is prevented from leaving the house or yard.

Passing On Information

A former Confederate signal officer, E.P. Alexander, gave an example of the amateur way in which Civil War spies of both sides operated. He explained how he communicated with a Confederate agent, Captain Pliny Bryan, in Washington in September 1861:

"Bryan was in Washington city, and was selecting a suitable room to rent, not on Pennsylvania Avenue, but in an elevated part of the city, from which Munson's Hill [near Alexandria, Virginia, which the Confederates then held] could be seen. He was taking the bearing of the hill by compass from his window, and [would] communicate it to us by an agreed-upon advertisement in a daily paper, which we received regularly. This would give us the bearing on which to turn our powerful telescope, loaned for the purpose by a Charleston gentleman, and in position on Munson's Hill.

"Then we would identify his window by finding a coffeepot in it, and by motions of the coffeepot, and opening and shutting the blinds, etc., he sent his messages, and we would reply, if necessary, by a large flag and by firing guns."

Pauline Cushman was an actress who spied for the Union. She followed the Confederate army and sent information back to the Union authorities.

Curriculum Context

Why might former slaves have been so willing to spy for the Union?

Such efficient spying was helped by the fact that the Confederacy could gain huge amounts of information from simply reading Northern newspapers, which were not censored. Similarly, the Union gained information from the Southern papers. Confederate General Braxton Bragg is said to have changed his tactics at Chickamauga, Tennessee, in 1863 because he read the Union battle plan in the *New York Times*.

Female spies

Women were some of the most successful spies on both sides. Some, like Rose O'Neal Greenhow, were of high social position, which gave them the opportunity to gain information by charming enemy officers.

The most effective female Union spy was Elizabeth Van Lew, who operated in Richmond, but there were many others, including the actress Pauline Cushman. She gained the confidence of Southern officers by toasting Confederate President Jefferson Davis on stage, for which she was fired. She then stayed with the Confederate army and gathered useful information to send to the Union authorities.

Although the punishment for spying was execution, female spies were not hanged if caught. In practice, many other spies were also only imprisoned.

Many escaped slaves also spied for the Union. They could get close to sources of information because as servants their presence was ignored by officials and officers discussing war matters. John Scobell was an effective black agent employed by Pinkerton in the Union secret service. Harriet Tubman, better known for her prewar work on the Underground Railroad helping runaway slaves to freedom, also spied for the Union during the war. The Union authorities also had access to the extensive informal information networks that existed among blacks in the South.

Flags

Flags are symbols of identity, representing shared history and group pride; as such, they took on enormous importance during the Civil War. Each army unit had its own flag, and individual generals had their own identifying flags.

In the Civil War men died for their flag. One of the first Union heroes of the war was Colonel Elmer Ellworth, gunned down in May 1861 for hauling down a secessionist flag in Alexandria, Virginia. In New Orleans a year later the Union governor Benjamin Butler ordered a Confederate loyalist to be hanged for tearing down the Stars and Stripes from a government building.

Curriculum Context

It might be interesting to investigate how armies teach recruits to be so loyal to a symbol such as a flag.

The national flags

The most important flags were the national flags of the two sides. The United States' flag went through three changes in design during the war years. The U.S. flag of 1861 bore 33 stars—this version of the Stars and Stripes flew over Fort Sumter when the war began on April 12. The 34-star flag came into being on July 4, 1861, with the entry of Kansas into the Union. In 1863 the 35-star flag was introduced after the statehood of West Virginia in June. This U.S. flag saw out the war.

One of the most unusual features of U.S. flags from this period is the variety of arrangements given to the stars. It was not until 1912 that the horizontal rows of stars familiar today were ordered by law. In the 1860s many flag makers arranged them in decorative patterns, such as in one big star.

The Confederacy had the task of creating a new national flag. In the opening months of the rebellion before the Confederate Congress came to a decision about the design, it was the flags of the seceded states

A Union soldier holds a tattered regimental Stars and Stripes belonging to the 8th Pennsylvania Reserves.

that symbolized Southern independence. The Mississippi flag, a single white, five-pointed star on a blue ground, became famous throughout the South as the "Bonnie Blue Flag" in a popular patriotic song. Jefferson Davis was sworn in as president of the provisional Confederate government in Montgomery on February 18, 1861, under the state flag of Alabama.

Versions of the Confederate flag

The first national flag of the Confederacy was adopted by Congress on March 4, 1861. Named the "Stars and Bars," it had one broad white stripe running the width of the flag across a field of red and in the top left-hand quarter—the area called the canton—there was a circle of seven five-pointed white stars on a field of blue. The seven stars represented the seven Southern states that

Canton

The vocabulary used to describe flags comes from heraldry.

had seceded by March 1861: South Carolina, Mississippi, Florida, Alabama, Georgia, Louisiana, and Texas. Four more stars were added after Virginia, Arkansas, Tennessee, and North Carolina seceded in April and May. Confederate troops carried this flag into battle at the First Battle of Bull Run on July 21, 1861.

This version was used until May 1863, when the second national flag was adopted. Called the "Stainless Banner," it was plain white and featured a blue St. Andrew's cross on a red ground bearing 13 white stars in the canton. The stars represented the 11 original Confederate states plus the border states of Kentucky and Missouri. The Stainless Banner was first used at the funeral of Stonewall Jackson in Richmond, Virginia, on May 11, 1863. It was adopted as the ensign of the Confederate navy in the same month.

The last pattern of Confederate national flag was introduced only five weeks before the end of the war. The Stainless Banner, being dominated by white, could easily be mistaken for a flag of surrender, and by the end of 1864 there were moves in congress to have it replaced. Congress finally adopted the third pattern in March 1865. The new version differed from the Stainless Banner only In having a broad band of red along the outer edge of the white ground. Few of this third version were ever made.

The national flags were used by some generals in the Army of Northern Virginia as their personal standards. The cavalry commander J.E.B. Stuart used the Stainless Banner, while Robert E. Lee flew the first pattern Stars and Bars with the stars arranged in a distinctive crescent formation.

Regimental colors
To the soldiers on the battle line their company or regimental flag, known as a color, symbolized the life of

Standard
A long, tapering flag that belongs to an individual or organization; standards were carried on long poles to act as rallying points on the battlefield.

Three versions of the
Confederate flag.
The Stars and Bars
(top) was the first
version. The Stainless
Banner (middle) was
used from May 1863
until March 1865.
The last flag was
introduced only
weeks before the
war's end.

Curriculum Context

The regiment was
important because army
commanders found it
easier to get men to be
loyal to their immediate
colleagues than to ideas
such as patriotism.

the unit and was a reminder of the homes they were fighting for. An important part of the mustering-in of volunteer regiments was the presentation of their flag, as Private Sam Watkins of the 1st Tennessee Infantry remembered in 1861: "Flags made by the ladies were presented to companies, and [then those present heard] the young orators tell how they should protect the flag, and that they would come back with the flag or come back not at all."

In action the flag was protected by a color guard of the regiment's most experienced noncommissioned officers and was a rallying point in the confusion of battle. Its very importance to the morale of a regiment drew enemy fire, and to capture a flag meant honor to the soldier who achieved it and disgrace to the unit that lost it.

In the Union armies infantry regiments carried two colors: the U.S. flag and a regimental color, which usually featured a bald eagle on a dark blue ground, the name of the regiment, and battle honors. The flags were large, 6 feet by 6 feet 6 inches (183cm by 198cm) and made of silk. They were sometimes decorated with a gold fringe. Cavalry and artillery regiments only carried a regimental color, but the Stars and Stripes was on their company or battery guidons, which were swallow-tailed pennants about 25 inches (63cm) long.

The battle flag

A Confederate regiment only carried one flag, which was smaller than its Union counterpart. Known as the battle flag, it was 48 in sq (122cm sq) for infantry, 30 in sq (76cm sq) for cavalry, and 36 in sq (91cm sq) for artillery. Made usually of wool, it carried the blue St. Andrew's cross on a red ground and 13 stars of the Southern states. Like Union regimental colors, the battle flag was decorated with battle honors. The battle flag has proved to be an enduring symbol of the South.

Impressment

As inflation in the Confederacy soared and money lost value, the government turned to taxing its people in goods and impressing (seizing) whatever it needed to fight the war, including food, animals, clothes, and slaves.

The act that gave the Confederate government the right to impress private property was passed on March 6, 1863. All private property could be impressed by the army (breeding livestock was later exempted).

Impressment officers could seize cattle, clothing, food, horses, iron, railroads, slaves, and even freedmen. Compensation for the impressed property was set by a price schedule and by two independent parties, one chosen by the impressment officer, the other by the property owner. Impressment of freedmen was like a draft—the laborers were compensated with an established minimum wage.

Response to impressment

The Confederate law of March 1863 legalized what army units already did. Nevertheless the law was widely unpopular. Many Southern governors complained that impressment violated state and individual rights. In spring 1863 the Confederate government took another unpopular measure to sustain the army, passing a 10 percent "tax in kind" on farm produce. Southerners regarded this as impressment under another name.

Opposition to impressment grew in the last months of the war, when the price schedule was abandoned. Impressment officers needed only to give a "just price" for goods. The "just price" took no account of the rapid inflation of Confederate currency. Many people believed it allowed officers to make personal profit.

Curriculum Context

How did impressment fit with the South's commitment to preserve states' rights, which was one of the major reasons for Secession.

Lost Cause

The Lost Cause was a particular set of beliefs about the causes and events of the Civil War that idealized life in the prewar Old South and explained, in a way that Southerners found acceptable, how the Confederacy lost the war.

Curriculum Context

If you are studying Reconstruction in the South, the Lost Cause is an important indication of how Southerners felt immediately after the war.

The Lost Cause myth developed among Southerners coming to terms with defeat. It gave them a way to retain their self-respect. The phrase "Lost Cause" was first used by Edward A. Pollard as the title of his 1866 history, which presented the Confederacy as a valiant institution brought low by an unfeeling enemy. It became a shorthand expression for a collective memory of what the Old South had stood for and the sacrifices it had made to defend its unique way of life.

Key beliefs

Several key beliefs shaped the myth. One was that slavery had not been the cause of the war but a smokescreen for unprovoked aggression by the North. Rather, the war was a struggle for states' rights. Far from being rebels, the Southerners were patriots, the true defenders of the Constitution. Those who believed in the Lost Cause refused to acknowledge that slavery had been an abuse of human rights. They developed a vision of the Old South as an idyllic rural society in which humane masters had lived in harmony with contented slaves. Popular novels reinforced this idea.

Idyllic

A view that depicts rural life as peaceful and contented.

Another key Lost Cause theme was that Confederate defeat had been inevitable because the South faced impossible odds. According to this version of events, the North's overwhelming superiority in manpower and industry was bound to prevail even though the Confederacy had better leaders and braver soldiers. Confederate generals Robert E. Lee and Thomas "Stonewall" Jackson were venerated almost as saints.

Holidays, monuments, and the setting up of patriotic organizations marked the sacrifice of the dead and veteran soldiers, and reinforced the Lost Cause myth.

Role in Reconstruction

The Lost Cause myth shaped how former Confederate states developed after the war. For one thing, it helped justify the terrorist activities of racist organizations such as the Ku Klux Klan. For many Southerners, the Klansmen were freedom fighters defending citizens against interfering Northerners and former slaves. Once federal troops left the South in 1877, the Lost Cause myth justified the creation of a racially segregated society. The rights of African Americans were gradually suppressed in the late 19th century.

Curriculum Context

Does the fact that the Lost Cause was used to justify racism mean that it had no value?

National reconciliation

Gradually, Northerners began to acknowledge the sacrifices of the South. For the sake of reconciliation the heroism of the soldiers of both sides was emphasized, rather than the root causes of the war. By the beginning of the 20th century Civil War commemorations had taken on a national flavor.

Reconciliation

To restore former enemies to a state of friendship, for example by agreeing to disagree over their differences.

The Lost Cause version of events became more acceptable. People in the North and the South flocked to see D. W. Griffith's silent movie *Birth of a Nation* (1915), which put a favorable gloss on Southern resistance to Reconstruction and showed the Ku Klux Klan in a positive light. Margaret Mitchell's bestselling novel *Gone With the Wind* (1936) became a hugely successful movie. The storyline was another version of the Lost Cause myth, a soft-focus look at plantation life.

The civil rights struggles of the 1950s and 1960s witnessed perhaps the last outpouring of Lost Cause sentiments, since many who resisted civil rights justified their stance in language reminiscent of the Lost Cause myth.

Mascots

Keeping animals as mascots was popular among army units of North and South. A surprising variety of animals were adopted. The animals lived in camp, traveled with the men on the march, and shared the hardships and dangers.

The presence of an animal mascot in the ranks came to identify many regiments as clearly as their regimental colors. Dogs were the most widely kept mascots, for their loyalty and hardiness. Care and welfare of animals often proved important to the morale of the soldiers.

Pets and strays

Many animal mascots began their army lives as pets kept by individual soldiers or as strays that wandered into camp. The 11th Pennsylvania, for example, adopted a Staffordshire bull terrier called Sallie, which was given to one of its officers as a puppy. She was wounded once by enemy action. Sallie was with the Union men at Gettysburg in July 1863, but was killed in February 1865 during the Battle of Hatcher's Run, Virginia. She was was buried on the battlefield. The soldiers felt the loss so deeply that an image of Sallie appears on the 11th Pennsylvania's memorial, which stands on the Gettysburg battlefield site.

The monument to the Union Irish Brigade at Gettysburg features an Irish wolfhound, the mascot of the 69th New York. The regiment adopted two of these dogs. On dress parade days the dogs were decked out in specially made green coats. An image of a wolfhound also appeared on the regimental flag.

Captured mascots

Some dog mascots followed their regiments into captivity. Frank, the mascot of the 2nd Kentucky, went into prison when the regiment was captured in 1862.

Curriculum Context

When studying soldiers' experience of the war, it might be useful to consider why they became so emotionally attached to the animals that acted as their mascots.

The dog was paroled with the rest of the unit after six months. Jack, a bull terrier with the 102nd Pennsylvania, was captured twice by the Confederates in Virginia. The second time he was returned after being exchanged for a Confederate soldier.

Unusual animals

Some regiments chose less common mascots. Units seemed to enjoy the notoriety a mascot gave them within the army. The 43rd Mississippi, for example, picked up a camel somewhere on their travels and named it Old Douglas. They became known to other Confederates as the "Camel Regiment." Old Douglas stayed with the Mississippi soldiers until it was killed by a Union sharpshooter at the Siege of Vicksburg in 1863.

On the Union side the 9th Connecticut Infantry kept a trained pig, which they called Jeff Davis as an insult to the Confederate president. The 2nd Rhode Island went to war with a sheep named Dick (until they ate it), while the 12th Wisconsin Infantry kept a tame bear. Wisconsin regiments routinely adopted unusual mascots. There was the tame racoon of the 12th Wisconsin, the badger kept by the 23rd Wisconsin, and probably the most famous Civil War mascot of all, the bald eagle of the 8th Wisconsin, Old Abe.

Parole
To release prisoners on a promise that they will not reoffend.

Camel
Camels had been introduced to the United States by the U.S. Army in the 1850s to carry baggage trains in the desert: the experiment was not very successful.

Old Abe

An eagle was presented to the 8th Wisconsin Regiment when the regiment first mustered in Wisconsin. It accompanied the regiment into 42 battles and engagements through Tennessee and Georgia. The eagle became known as Old Abe for President Abraham Lincoln. In action Old Abe was tethered to a large wooden perch decorated with a painted Union shield, carried by a soldier known as the eagle bearer. On occasions Old Abe would be set loose to fly above the fighting, and he became so well known that Confederates called him "the Yankee Buzzard." Despite Confederate efforts to kill or capture him, the bird stayed with the 8th Wisconsin until September 1864, when he was retired. He was presented to the state of Wisconsin and housed in the state capitol.

Medals and Honors

At the beginning of the war neither the Union nor the Confederacy had a system of military decorations for valor. This remained the case in the Confederacy, but in 1861 the Union authorized the Medal of Honor for gallantry in action.

Enlisted men on both sides could be recognized for bravery in several ways. They might be "mentioned in dispatches" to headquarters by their commanding officers. Many commanders also made it a practice to name in their battle reports soldiers who had performed with conspicuous bravery. The Confederate Congress published a "Roll of Honor" listing men cited for bravery and could also issue "Thanks of the Confederate Congress" to individual soldiers.

Awarding brevets

Officers enjoyed more recognition. They, too, were mentioned in dispatches or in battle reports. They were also eligible for brevet promotions. Brevet ranks were temporary, honorary ranks but carried no pay or authority. Thus an officer could hold two ranks, his official rank and a temporary brevet rank earned for gallantry. The Union army conferred brevet ranks often. The Confederate army had provisions to make brevet promotions, but did not award any.

The Medal of Honor was created in 1861 and intended only to last for the duration of the war. In 1863 Congress voted to make it permanent. The Medal of Honor remains the highest award for valor in the United States.

Medal of Honor

President Abraham Lincoln created in December 1861 the nation's first medal for gallantry in action, a "medal of honor" for U.S. Navy and Marine Corps enlisted men. The government extended the award to army enlisted men in July 1862 and to army officers in March 1863.

The Union army awarded a total of 1,195 Medals of Honor during the war to 1,194 individual officers and men. The first army Medals of Honor were presented by

Secretary of War Edwin M. Stanton on March 25, 1863. Some medals were backdated to honor acts of bravery near the beginning of the war.

Sergeant William H. Carney of the 54th Massachusetts Infantry was the first African American to earn a Medal of Honor. A total of 16 African American enlisted men won the Medal of Honor during the war, adding luster to their already commendable combat record.

Curriculum Context

Medals are often seen as part of the apparatus that helps maintain soldiers' morale and their loyalty to the army.

Confederate medals

The Confederate government awarded only one medal for bravery. It was issued to the 49 members of an artillery battery known as the Davis Guard when they prevented a Union landing in Texas on September 8, 1863. After the war Confederate organizations raised funds to issue medals to veterans. In 1900 the United Daughters of the Confederacy issued the Southern Cross of Honor to Confederate veterans, giving out 12,500 crosses in one year. In 1977 the Sons of Confederate Veterans issued a Confederate Medal of Honor, which was awarded posthumously for bravery.

The Medal Purge of 1917

The Union Medal of Honor, although originally intended to honor acts of extraordinary bravery, was also awarded for many routine battlefield actions. Union recruiting officers frequently used them as rewards to encourage enlistment. This widespread distortion of the original intent of the Medal of Honor led the U.S. Army to revoke 911 medals in 1917. That included 864 presented to the members of one regiment, the 27th Maine Infantry, for standing ready to defend Washington, D.C., against a possible Confederate attack in July 1863. The commission also revoked the only Medal of Honor ever awarded to a woman, Dr. Mary Edwards Walker, who assisted Union army surgeons during the war. Walker continued to wear her medal, however, and President Jimmy Carter formally reinstated it in 1977. Although several Union states minted and issued medals for gallantry, the Congressional Medal of Honor, along with brevet ranks and rolls of honor, remained the primary Union recognition of bravery in battle. The Medal of Honor continues in use to this day, while the last brevet rank was awarded in 1918.

Medicine

With its huge armies and deadly weapons, the Civil War has often been described as the first modern war. Unfortunately for the participants, however, medical care and surgical treatment remained for the most part primitive.

Bacteria

Tiny microscopic animals that transmit disease.

In the 1860s the existence of bacteria and viruses was still undiscovered. Surgeons operated with dirty instruments in filthy conditions, so even when injured soldiers had bullets removed or wounds sewed up, they were likely to face deadly infections. Combat wounds were not the greatest killers, however. Disease took far more lives, and it created a huge problem that neither side in the war was able to solve.

When the war began in 1861, the United States army had only 113 surgeons in its ranks, 24 of whom resigned to support the Confederacy. Some doctors had attended medical schools, but many others had simply studied with other doctors and lacked the most basic knowledge of treating illness or injury.

Curriculum Context

Although medical schools had been established, many doctors in the United States had only unofficial qualifications.

The Army Medical Bureau

For the Union, medical matters fell under the authority of the Army Medical Bureau. In April 1862 the bureau was taken over by 33-year-old William A. Hammond. He expanded its size and improved its professionalism.

Meanwhile, the Confederates had to build a medical service from nothing. The Confederate Medical Department was established by Samuel Preston Moore, who recruited doctors and nurses, set up procedures, founded hospitals, and eventually created a medical service similar to that of the Union. Moore's task, though, was hampered by shortages caused by the Union blockade. Given the circumstances, Moore created an effective medical department.

Unhealthy troops

Many recruits in both armies were physically unfit, especially as both sides became desperate for manpower. However, commanders soon learned that unfit troops were not merely useless; caring for them took away resources from the military effort. In 1862 an investigation in the Union army found that 25 percent of the soldiers were unfit for military duty.

The greatest threat to a soldier was disease. Historians estimate that disease killed at least twice as many soldiers as combat wounds. That would mean that of the 620,000 soldiers who died in the Civil War, around 207,000 died from wounds and 413,000 from disease.

Disease had a direct effect on military campaigns. The Union's first attempt to take the city of Vicksburg in Mississippi in 1862 failed largely because more than half the troops were sick. Disease also figured in Lincoln's decision to abandon the Peninsular Campaign in Virginia that same year.

Curriculum Context

The poor medical quality of most recruits mirrored the poor health of many parts of American society. What reasons might there be for that?

Killer Diseases

The greatest killer of the war was probably dysentery (severe diarrhea). Nobody knew that dysentery was caused by bacteria, although some doctors suspected that there was a relationship between the cleanliness of army camps and the disease. Most soldiers gave little thought to using a nearby river as both a latrine and a drinking-water source. Simply boiling water before drinking it would have killed off the bacteria and saved countless lives, but nobody knew that. However, even when army doctors and officers instructed their men where best to place latrines, the men often disregarded their instructions.

Rivaling dysentery in deadliness were the diseases typhoid and pneumonia, which were even harder to prevent. A fourth major cause of death was the mosquito-borne disease malaria, which was particularly severe in the South in the summertime.

Some diseases, like measles, mumps, and chicken pox, might not kill very many men but could cause such widespread sickness that they could make a company, a regiment, or an entire army unfit for duty. Sexually transmitted diseases such as gonorrhea and syphilis were another widespread problem.

Fatal treatments

The most common treatment for many diseases was calomel. However, calomel depleted the body's vital fluids—already a major problem in diarrhea—and in large doses it could cause mercury poisoning. Many soldiers tried to avoid seeing a doctor unless they were near death. One of the few effective drugs available was quinine, which could prevent and treat malaria.

A wound often meant death or the loss of a limb. Muskets fired large lead bullets that caused terrible wounds. Soldiers with a head or gut wound were often left for dead. For arm and leg wounds amputation was common to prevent gangrene infection. Some wounded solders were treated by a surgeon supplied with anesthetics such as chloroform or ether, which made operations more bearable. Those less lucky could expect only whiskey and a bullet to bite on for the pain. Opium was also widely used as a painkiller.

Sanitary Commission

The Union's medical efforts were greatly assisted by a civilian volunteer agency known as the U.S. Sanitary Commission. Founded in June 1861, the commission

Soldiers wounded in the Civil War recovering in a hospital. The cramped conditions and lack of basic hygiene meant that many hospitals were breeding grounds for diseases that were as much a threat to life as the patient's original wounds.

Amputation at a Field Infirmary

From Bell Irvin Wile's book *The Life of Johnny Reb*:

"I then went back to the field infirmary where I saw large numbers of wounded lying on the ground as thick as a drove of hogs in a log ... those shot in the bowels were crying for water.

Jake Fellers had his arm amputated without chloroform. I held the artery and Dr. Huot cut if off by candle light. We continued to operate until late at night ... I was very tired and slept on the ground."

was intended to investigate and advise on medical matters. Soon, however, its thousands of volunteers were raising money to buy bandages, medicine, and other necessities. Its inspectors tried to educate soldiers to keep their camps clean and healthy. The commission also trained thousands of nurses and pushed the government to build more hospitals. It worked closely with a new unit of the Union army, the Ambulance Corps, which evacuated wounded soldiers from the front lines. Many of the commission's practices were adopted by the Confederate Medical Department.

Women nurses

Work as nurses gave women their most direct role in the Civil War. At the start of the war most nurses were still men, but by its end some 3,200 women had served as nurses in the Union army. The Confederacy was slower to use female nurses and used fewer, but it also used slave women as nurses. Some women, like Clara Barton, who later founded the American Red Cross, simply worked as nurses on their own.

The war's main contributions to medicine were to train a new generation of surgeons and to open up the nursing profession to women. It also led to the creation of an ambulance corps. However, it was not until the 20th century that scientists began to understand the causes of many diseases and infections, and to develop effective treatments for them.

> **Curriculum Context**
>
> Many curricula expect students to understand changes the war made to the roles of women.

> **Curriculum Context**
>
> Medical developments were among the most influential scientific innovations of the Civil War.

Memorials and Souvenirs

Many Civil War soldiers took souvenirs from the battlefield to mark their experiences, while later generations have remembered the war with memorial ceremonies and by dedicating monuments to honor the dead.

Memorial Day

On the first Memorial Day flowers were laid on the graves of both Union and Confederate soldiers in Arlington Cemetery, in Virginia just outside Washington, D.C.

Curriculum Context

Many communities in the United States have monuments to the Civil War dead. It might be interesting to discover where your closest ones are.

Soldiers began creating memorials even before the war ended. Union officers built a monument at Manassas, Virginia, in 1864, the first Civil War battle site to be marked in this way. In the South women's groups began decorating the graves of the Confederate dead with flowers. This practice developed into an official Memorial Day, first observed in 1868.

Healing wounds

For those who survived the war memorials were a symbol of all they sacrificed. From 1865 to 1885 Southerners placed most of their monuments in cemeteries. After 1885 both Northerners and Southerners tended to place memorials on the battlefields themselves. Gettysburg, Pennsylvania, the site of the war's largest battle, served as a natural focus of remembrance. The site is filled with obelisks, grand amphitheaters, and realistic statues of fighting men.

Building monuments

Building monuments in the postwar period was often divisive. Monument unveiling days in the South became a focus of resistance to Republican policies. In Richmond, Virginia, on October 26, 1875, nearly 50,000 people attended the unveiling of General Thomas "Stonewall" Jackson's monument. The day included speeches calling for the end of Reconstruction.

Battlefield memorials

Beginning in the 1880s, the U.S. government initiated the process of turning the battlefields themselves into memorials by designating them national battlefields or national historical parks. This takeover of the most prominent battlefields of the Civil War brought the process of remembrance under firm federal control.

In the 1870s Union general Daniel Sickles became the head of the New York State Monuments Commission. He played a key role in ensuring that the battlefield at Gettysburg was preserved as a memorial. He and others dictated the styles and placings of monuments at Gettysburg, and effectively prevented Confederate veterans' organizations from building monuments. Even today, most Confederate memorials are confined to one area of the battlefield, near the start line of the second and third days' attacks.

Curriculum Context

Should the government have a role in remembrance, given that the Confederates were actually fighting against the federal government?

Two capitals

Washington, D.C., and Richmond, Virginia, are filled with reminders of their Civil War past. Monuments and memorials dot the landscape of both cities, ensuring that residents and visitors alike never forget the war. In Washington more monuments exist to the Civil War than to any other single event; more equestrian statues

Equestrian statue

A statue that portrays its subject on horseback.

Souvenirs of the Surrender

On April 9, 1865, Union General Ulysses S. Grant and Confederate General Robert E. Lee met in the parlor of Wilmer McLean's house in Appomattox, Virginia, to agree the terms for the surrender of Lee's army. The occasion transformed McLean's parlor into a historic location. When the meeting was over, Union officers who were present carried away every item in the room. General Philip Sheridan secured the small oval desk on which Grant wrote out the surrender terms and later presented it to General George Armstrong Custer.

Other officers cleaned out everything else, paying McLean for some items and simply stealing others. When everything else was gone, a staff officer made off with the room's carpet and a rag doll belonging to McLean's daughter. The doll remained in the officer's family for years after the war. Other observers who were not present at the conference dismantled the porch railings of the McLean house, and a Pennsylvania soldier carried off the seal of Appomattox County from the courthouse.

A monument to the Confederate dead at Hollywood Cemetery in Richmond, Virginia. The 90-ft (27-m) high pyramid was built in 1869. Many Confederate bodies were removed from the battlefields around Richmond and reinterred at Hollywood.

stand there than in any other city in the United States. In addition, the Lincoln Memorial stands as a tribute to the wartime commander-in-chief.

Richmond's Hollywood Cemetery contains numerous memorials to Confederate officers and soldiers. Monument Avenue has a succession of memorials to the most famous Confederate generals from Virginia. They include the "Stonewall" Jackson monument and others to Robert E. Lee and J.E.B. Stuart.

Silent reminders

A memorial statue of a Civil War soldier stands in most small American towns, especially those in the South. These monuments commemorate the local men who went to war. A monument at the University of North Carolina, affectionately known as "Silent Sam," remembers the students who fought. Such silent reminders ensure that Americans will never forget the cost of their Civil War.

Curriculum Context

Do you think that physical memorials are necessary to remind people about the war, or is the war established enough in Americans' minds not to require reminders?

Military Academies

Military academies contributed much to the Civil War, especially the U.S. Military Academy at West Point, which trained more than 1,000 officers on both sides. On several occasions graduates found themselves fighting their former classmates.

President Thomas Jefferson had set up the first national military school, the U.S. Military Academy at West Point, New York, in 1802, to train military engineers. In 1812, however, the academy was reorganized to become the main training facility for U.S. Army officers.

The Norwich system

A number of military schools were founded before the Civil War. Alden Partridge, a West Point graduate, founded a military academy in Norwich, Vermont, in 1819. The American Literary, Scientific, and Military Academy (now Norwich University) became a model for other military academies. It combined instruction in

Curriculum Context

The fact that officers on both sides of the war had been to the same military academies meant that they often used the same or similar tactics.

The Virginia Military Institute

The Virginia Military Institute (VMI) was established at the state arsenal at Lexington, Virginia, in 1839. The school had the greatest impact on the Civil War of all of the country's military academies apart from West Point.

Its wartime superintendent, Francis H. Smith (a West Point graduate), supported the Confederate war effort by offering his cadets as drillmasters for newly formed volunteer regiments. The future Confederate General Thomas "Stonewall" Jackson, then a little-known instructor at VMI, led the cadets to Richmond in 1861 for this purpose. Although Jackson was not

himself a VMI graduate, he was to be forever associated with the school.

Two hundred VMI cadets fought at the Battle of New Market, Virginia, in May 1864—the only time a group of students fought as a unit in battle. They suffered 20 percent casualties. In total, VMI produced 20 generals, 90 colonels, and hundreds of junior officers for Confederate armies. In retaliation for the role of VMI cadets at New Market and the school's contribution to the Confederate cause, Union General David Hunter burned down the school in June 1864. VMI was rebuilt after the war.

arts and humanities with sciences and military training. Academy students wore uniforms, observed a military chain of command, and drilled with weapons.

Southern military academies

Several Southern military academies were set up as a result of the militia system, under which states maintained arsenals of weapons for use by militia units. State governments established military academies next to arsenals, thus providing guards for the equipment and weapons for use in military training. Examples include the famous Virginia Military Institute (VMI), established at the state arsenal in Lexington.

West Point graduates

The U.S. Military Academy at West Point contributed more than 1,000 officers to the Civil War armies, in roughly equal proportion to each side. Of the 425 Confederate general-level officers, 146 were West Point graduates, compared to 217 of the 583 Union generals. Confederate President Jefferson Davis was also a West Point graduate.

The Citadel, one of the military academies established at a state arsenal, can be seen in the middle distance of this view of Charleston, South Carolina, with the arsenal behind it.

Military Bands

Military bands were very important to the armies of the Civil War. Music not only raised the morale of the troops, but soldiers marched better and longer to a rousing tune. And bands provided entertainment in camp in the evenings.

The connection between music and soldiering was close. Not only were orders issued and passed by means of bugle and drum calls, but it was recognized that music boosted soldiers' morale in battle. Military bands were an official part of a regiment's organization.

Before the war U.S. Army regulations, which were later also adopted by the Confederacy, stated that an infantry regiment could enlist a band of 16 musicians, while each cavalry troop was permitted to enlist two musicians, which in an average cavalry regiment meant a mounted band of at least 20 men.

Aid to recruitment

Music also inspired volunteers to enlist. When the states of North and South issued their calls to arms in April 1861, they were made to the sound of patriotic tunes like "Bonnie Blue Flag" or "Yankee Doodle." Recruiting officers made it a high priority to bring town or militia bands into their new regiments.

In 1862 the Union army decided that it could no longer afford regimental bands and discharged the musicians from service. However, brigades were still permitted to keep bands, and many musicians simply reenlisted to serve in them.

Musical instruments

Most bands played brass instruments, accompanied by drums and other percussion instruments. Woodwind instruments like clarinets tended to be too fragile for

Morale
The positive quality that makes men willing to perform difficult tasks such as fighting, even in the face of huge odds.

army service, but fifes—a type of small flute—were widely used. Some regiments replaced their brass bands with corps of fifes and drums.

The musical repertoire of the bands varied greatly. Most bands did not only play marches but could turn their hands to dance music such as polkas and waltzes, as well as sentimental ballads and patriotic songs. That was important because their role in the regiments was not restricted to playing on the battlefield. Bands were essential as a source of entertainment to the soldiers in camp, and concerts were highly popular.

The quality of the music the bands produced also seems to have varied widely. The Confederates generally had the reputation of being musicians who played with more enthusiasm than skill or talent.

However, the band of the Union 6th Wisconsin regiment had the reputation of being the worst military band of the whole war. The band could play only one song and was so poor at playing it that the regiment's commanding officer sent men to serve in the band as a punishment.

Curriculum Context

When describing soldier life, remember that for most of the time they were not fighting, so entertainment such as concerts was vital to prevent boredom.

An African American military brass band, photographed in Washington in 1865. Brass instruments were the preferred instruments of most military bands during the Civil War.

Morale

In wartime high morale can lead to great achievements, and low morale can have a disastrous effect on citizens and soldiers. In the Civil War both the Union and the Confederacy used a variety of methods to enhance and sustain enthusiasm.

Morale among the fighting men of both sides was very high for the first months of the Civil War. Most soldiers enlisted voluntarily and viewed war as both a glorious adventure and a patriotic duty. Union and Confederate soldiers thought that the war would be very short, a notion ended by such bloody early encounters as First Bull Run (July 1861) and Shiloh (April 1862). After both sides realized that the war would be long, devotion to cause and comrades helped sustain soldier morale.

Boosting morale

Through 1862 and 1863, leaders turned to a variety of methods to improve morale. Both sides instituted various rewards, as well as systems for furlough (home leave). Leave was granted to reward reenlistment and as a balance to conscription, introduced in the South in 1862 and in the North in 1863. The chance to see friends and family raised spirits, as did regular pay, good equipment, and tolerable living conditions. Religious practices also helped maintain high morale.

Victory on the battlefield

The greatest factor in the morale of any army, however, is victory. Battlefield success can reduce the effect of other negative factors on troop spirit. The Union Army of the Potomac, for example, the Civil War's best fed, clothed, and supplied fighting force, suffered from low morale through much of the war because it endured a string of defeats at the hands of General Robert E. Lee. After a monumental victory at Gettysburg in July 1863 the army's morale improved rapidly.

Curriculum Context

Other rewards included medals and brevet ranks, or temporary, honorary, promotions.

Conversely, Lee's Confederate Army of Northern Virginia was known for consistently high morale in spite of shortages of food, clothing, and equipment, and sporadic pay, as it dealt its Union enemy defeat after defeat. Only in late 1864 and 1865 did a costly siege at Petersburg combine with shortages and battlefield defeats to erode the morale of Lee's army.

Civilian morale

High morale was also important on the home front, since a happy populace produced more food and war material, and family members could either help or harm troop spirits. Citizens on both sides made an effort to keep up morale. For example, they circulated stories of heroism by their own troops and criminal acts by their enemy, and held patriotic fund-raising events. The Confederate home front was particularly affected by the war because most battles were fought on Southern soil. Difficult economic conditions also lowered civilian morale in the South.

Demoralizing the South

Low civilian morale appears to have contributed to increased desertion in Confederate armies from late 1864, as William T. Sherman's "March to the Sea" cut a swath of destruction through Georgia. Families who had suffered the absence of loved ones for three years or more reached breaking point. They wrote letters begging their husbands and brothers to come home, making it clear that they considered the soldiers' obligations to the failing Confederacy at an end.

To this day historians debate the cause of the collapse of Confederate resistance. Did battlefield defeat lead to low troop and civilian morale, or did a failure of will at home lead to military defeat? There is evidence to support both claims. It is clear, however, that morale was important both in stretching the war into four years of bloodshed and in leading to Union victory.

Curriculum Context

If the curriculum asks you to summarize the reasons for Confederate defeat, which would you count as more significant, military defeat or a collapse of morale?

Music

Music was a constant companion to the fighting men of both sides in the Civil War. Musicians accompanied units into battle and on the march, while at home songs bolstered patriotism and encouraged contributions to the war efforts.

Military music of the Civil War came in a variety of forms. Field musicians such as fifers, drummers, and buglers marched with fighting units. Union army regulations called for each regiment to field one fifer and drummer per company of 100 men, supervised by the drum major. Field musicians were noncombatants and were often too young to enlist.

Fife
A small high-pitched flute, similar to a piccolo, most often used in marching bands.

Perhaps the most famous young Civil War musician was John Joseph "Johnny" Clem, who joined the 22nd Massachusetts Infantry in 1861 at the age of nine. Johnny Clem served as a drummer and messenger for the remainder of the war, was made a lieutenant in 1871, and retired as a brigadier general in 1915. He was the last Civil War veteran in the U.S. Army at the time of his retirement.

"Battle Hymn of the Republic"

In 1861 Julia Ward Howe wrote a poem for *Atlantic Monthly* magazine entitled "Battle Hymn of the Republic." Musician William Steffe then set the poem to the tune of "John Brown's Body," creating the most famous and enduring song of the Civil War:

Mine eyes have seen the glory
Of the coming of the Lord;
He is trampling out the vintage
Where the grapes of wrath are stored;
He hath loosed the fateful lightning
Of His terrible swift sword;
His truth is marching on.

Chorus
Glory! Glory! Hallelujah!
Glory! Glory! Hallelujah!
Glory! Glory! Hallelujah!
His truth is marching on.

Military bands

Many Civil War units also marched to battle accompanied by bands of professional musicians. More than 400 Union and 100 Confederate bands served regiments and brigades. These bands of brass, percussion, and some woodwind instruments supplied recreational music in camp and played on special occasions. In battle, band members usually became stretcher bearers or hospital orderlies.

One of the most famous Confederate regimental bands belonged to the 26th North Carolina Infantry. Many of the band's members were Moravians, subscribers to a pacifist religious sect. They would not fight, but were conscripted in 1862 and enrolled into the band.

While field and band music was commonly heard in camp, informal singing and dancing were also popular pastimes. Soldiers enjoyed music provided by their more musical comrades on instruments such as banjos, fiddles, Jew's harps, and harmonicas. Popular ballads such as "Lorena" and "Home Sweet Home" helped soldiers while away the long hours of tedium in camp, helped to raise morale, and also served as an antidote to homesickness.

Civil War songs

Some of the most famous songs in American history were products of the Civil War. The lyrics of these songs encouraged patriotism and reminded Northerners and Southerners of their various reasons for fighting. The most famous Northern war song was "Battle Hymn of the Republic," a stirring anthem based on an older religious song (see box page 49).

A popular song in the South, "The Bonnie Blue Flag," highlighted the feelings of thousands of Southerners that the Lincoln administration wanted to subjugate them and deprive them of their rights and property.

Jew's harp

A musical instrument with a protruding metal tongue; the lyre-shaped instrument is held in the mouth by one hand and the tongue is plucked using the other hand.

Curriculum Context

Curricula might ask you to consider ways in which the Confederacy maintained its determination to defeat the North.

National Cemeteries

In July 1862 the Union began the process of purchasing land to be used as cemeteries for the Union dead. Today there are 120 national cemeteries serving as the final resting place of thousands of war dead and veterans.

Early in the war, neither government made large-scale plans for the burial of the war dead. The terrible battles of 1862 created a need for extensive burial grounds for dead soldiers. On July 17, 1862, Congress authorized President Abraham Lincoln to buy grounds to be turned into national cemeteries "for soldiers who shall have died in the service of their country."

Wartime cemeteries

The 1862 act established 14 cemeteries, mainly located near battlefields for ease of burial. One, located in Sharpsburg, Maryland, saw the interment of more than 4,000 Union dead from the Battle of Antietam. Lincoln established another national cemetery at Gettysburg, Pennsylvania, and helped dedicate it on November 19, 1863, with the Gettysburg Address, perhaps the most famous speech in American history.

Confederate soldiers, meanwhile, were buried where they fell or in public cemeteries or family plots. Late in the war the Confederate government commandeered private land for burials.

Postwar burials

In 1866 the U.S. government created a national cemetery system and made provisions for the Union dead to be reinterred in new cemeteries. Burial teams in the South located and reburied the remains of Union soldiers killed in battle and hastily buried. By 1870 nearly 300,000 Union dead were buried in 73 national cemeteries, although half of them were unidentified.

Curriculum Context

Does the Gettysburg Address help explain what might have been Lincoln's intention in setting up national cemeteries?

Commandeer

To seize private property for military use.

Arlington Cemetery in Virginia is situated on the former estate of Confederate General Robert E. Lee. The Union confiscated the land and buried 5,000 Union dead there between May 1864 and the end of the war.

Many people in the South were angered by the lack of federal provision for the burial of the Confederate dead. In response the Ladies' Memorial Association was formed to clean and decorate Confederate graves. In Southern cemeteries, private plot owners often donated their plots for military burials.

Burying veterans

In 1873 a new regulation decreed that along with those who had died in combat, all honorably discharged veterans were eligible to be buried in national cemeteries.

The Civil War origins of the nation's cemeteries are clearest at Arlington in Virginia. The land earmarked in 1864 for Arlington Cemetery once belonged to the wife of Confederate General Robert E. Lee. From the front porch of Arlington House the young Lee looked out over fields and woods that were confiscated by the Union during the Civil War and deliberately turned into a resting place for Union war dead.

Native American Participation

Around 20,000 Native Americans from many parts of the country participated in Civil War action. Some joined the Union army, while others supported the Confederacy. Many distinguished themselves as courageous fighters.

While many Native Americans saw the Civil War as irrelevant, others hoped that military service would help obtain a better deal for their people.

In the 1830s many Native Americans in the eastern states were subjected to compulsory removal to territories west of the Mississippi River as a result of the Indian Removal Act (1830), so few saw the federal government as an ally. A few Native Americans were themselves slave owners, but others saw parallels between the discrimination they faced and slavery.

The Cherokee Nation

The Cherokee Nation illustrated these contradictions. Before being forced to move to Oklahoma, some Cherokees in Georgia had owned slaves. By the outbreak of the Civil War the Cherokee in the west were divided. While Chief John Ross wanted to remain neutral, support for the Confederacy crystallized around Isaac Stand Watie. He was commissioned as a colonel in the Confederate army in October 1861 and commanded a battalion of Cherokee.

John Ross found himself in a difficult position: Most of the Cherokee's Native American neighbors backed the Confederacy, and on October 7, 1861, he reluctantly signed a treaty with the Confederate government. In return for 10 companies of mounted soldiers the Cherokee would be given protection, food, and a delegate to the Confederate Congress at Richmond, Virginia. After Ross's capture by Union troops, Colonel

Curriculum Context

Students might be asked to discuss Native American responses to the Civil War.

Curriculum Context

The different positions of John Ross and Stand Watie make the Cherokee a good case study in Native American reaction to the war.

Guerrilla

A soldier who fights by ambush, raids, and sabotage, rather than regular pitched battles.

Stand Watie took over as Principal Chief of the Cherokee and drafted all men between 18 and 50 into Confederate military service. Stand Watie proved to be a skillful guerrilla commander.

Support for the Union

Many peoples gave their backing to the Union. Early in 1862, Native Americans from—among others—the Delaware, Seminole, Creek, Seneca, Choctaw, and Chickasaw were organized in the 1st and 2nd Indian Home Guard. In Virginia and North Carolina the Pamunkey and Lumbee also backed the Union, and men of the Iroquois Nation joined the 5th Pennsylvania Volunteer Infantry.

The most famous Native American on the Union side was Ely Samuel Parker. Parker, a Seneca from Illinois, was unable to obtain a commission until summer 1863. By September he was on General Ulysses S. Grant's staff. He made the final draft of the terms of surrender signed at Appomattox Court House on April 9, 1865.

Fighting another war

During 1863 and 1864 Native Americans in the West fought another war as Union forces strove to control raiding parties of Apaches and other bands. Most of the action was in New Mexico and Minnesota. In the fall of 1864 settlers near Denver, Colorado, complained to the government about Native American raids. On November 29 Colonel John M. Chivington led 900 troops into a village of Arapaho and Cheyenne. They killed more than 150 men, women, and children in what became known as the Sand Creek Massacre.

Curriculum Context

What does the Sand Creek Massacre reveal about relations between Native Americans and white settlers in the West in the mid-1860s?

While the North's most famous Native American was present at Lee's surrender, the South's best-known Indian fighter initially refused to accept surrender. It was not until two months after Appomattox that Stand Watie finally surrendered to Union troops.

Newspapers and Reporters

Newspapers were the public's main source of information about the war. Thanks to the recently invented telegraph, news could be sent quickly back to the newspapers and then distributed widely by rail to eagerly waiting readers.

There had been an enormous increase in the number of newspapers published in the United States during the early 19th century. By 1861 there were almost 2,500 daily and weekly titles. The North had twice as many newspapers as the South and four times the average circulation. New York alone had 17 newspapers, of which the most important were the *Times*, the *Herald*, and the *Tribune*. Of all the newspapers published, 370 appeared daily—290 in the North and 80 in the South.

Political bias

All the papers took an openly political stand. They had no interest in the modern idea of balanced reporting. The only newspaper that made an attempt to be objective and even-handed was the *New York Times*, whose motto was "moderation in all things." Horace Greeley's *New York Tribune*, the *Chicago Tribune*, and the *Philadelphia Inquirer* took a Radical Republican stance. They supported the war as a way to achieve the abolition of slavery. More moderate Republican papers included the *New York Times* and the *Boston Journal*.

The Democrat papers in the North, such as the *Chicago Times* and the *Cincinnati Inquirer*, in general sought a negotiated settlement to the war and regarded the end of slavery as an obstacle, not a goal. The *New York Herald* was the leading Northern paper to take a completely independent stance. It supported the secession of the Southern states and opposed the war until 1862.

Curriculum Context

How might it have affected public opinion on the home front that news of the war was politically biased?

War correspondents

It took a large number of correspondents to cover the different theaters of the war. The *New York Herald* sent 63 reporters to cover the conflict. The *Times* and the *Tribune* sent more than 20 each. In all, Northern papers sent about 500 and Southern papers about 100 reporters to cover the war.

Newspapers hired artists to enliven their pages with images of the conflict. Drawings, rather than photographs, were used because there was not yet a method of reproducing photographs in newspapers. Drawings were turned into hardwood engravings from which thousands of copies could be printed.

The public was hungry for the latest news, made possible by the telegraph. "By Telegraph" became a

A *New York Herald* wagon and reporters in the field. The most widely read daily newspaper in New York, the *Herald* spent freely on coverage of the war, and sent 63 reporters to the battlefields.

common byline, and for the first time it was possible for people at home to read about events that had taken place just the previous day, rather than two weeks before. The *Cincinnati Commercial* summed up the situation in 1862, "The people want news more than they want victories."

The result was that reporters had to keep a steady supply of stories flowing in a bid to satisfy their editors. Inevitably, some reporters filed invented, inaccurate accounts. The reporting of a Union victory at Fredericksburg before the ultimate humiliating Confederate triumph was one of many examples.

Modest rewards

Reporters were modestly paid at between $10 and $25 a week, including expenses. Several found other ways of supplementing their income. Some used their inside knowledge of conditions concerning upcoming battles to successfully play the stock markets, gambling on what commodities might be in short supply. Albert Holmes Bodman of the *Chicago Tribune* covered the war for five months on a weekly salary of $16. When he returned home, he had made $22,000, largely from poker games and cotton running. The work could also be very dangerous. Irving Carson of the *Chicago Times* became the first reporter lost in action when he was decapitated by a cannonball in the Battle of Shiloh on April 6, 1862.

War correspondents worked hard to satisfy the demands of their editors and readership. After a long day gathering information on the battlefield, they wrote up their piece at night. Then, at dawn, they galloped to the nearest telegraph station in order to telegraph their story to the paper before racing back to start all over again. Competition among the many reporters in the North meant they had to keep up a relentless pace.

Expenses
The costs of living while working, such as the price of meals, lodging, and transportation.

Cotton running
Smuggling cotton out of the South through the Union blockade or over the border to Mexico.

Curriculum Context

The censorship of the press might be an interesting topic for students who are asked to evaluate Lincoln's view of civil liberties during the war.

Censorship

Every article sent to a newspaper in the North was subject to censorship since Union agents controlled the telegraph lines. The War Department did not want to be criticized or let the enemy get hold of any useful information. In the event, both sides gleaned valuable information by reading each others' newspapers. Perhaps for this reason army commanders disliked reporters and rarely helped them. Union General William T. Sherman went so far as to accuse them of "doing infinite mischief."

The Southern Press

Most Southern newspapers were weeklies, with relatively small circulations. As the Union troops went deeper south, they shut down many of the newspapers—the *Charleston Mercury* eventually became a single-sheet newspaper. The Southern newspapers were mainly Democrat in their views; but once the war started, all of them put the Southern cause before objective news reporting. Many of the Southern papers relied for information on the Press Association of Confederate States, formed after the South lost access to the Associated Press service in New York. The South also relied on officers supplying information via letter or telegraph and civilian correspondents. One civilian correspondent,

George W. Bagby, wrote for 23 Southern papers using various pseudonyms.

Southern correspondents often doubled up as soldiers, and many of them did other jobs as well as war reporting. The South's leading war correspondent, Peter Alexander, was a lawyer from Georgia who campaigned for better conditions for the ordinary soldier. Newspaper men, like other civilians, often had to fight for the cause. The editor of the Confederate newspaper in Macon, Georgia, wrote, "There was no paper issued from the Confederate office on Saturday morning. Every man in the establishment was in the field on Saturday. We hope our subscribers will consider this a sufficient excuse."

Nurses and Nursing

In 1860 the traditional view of women was that they were weak and timid, and would be quite unable to face the rigors of nursing wounded men straight from the battlefield. That attitude was to change during the Civil War.

The Civil War was different from earlier wars. It involved the entire population—both men and women. Earlier views of women as too delicate to be able to care for the wounded were discarded as women left their homes to travel hundreds of miles to nurse casualties.

Nursing required strength, stamina, and desensitization to the horrible sights and smells of hospitals and battlefields. Most doctors did not want women nurses at all—they thought women were not strong enough and would not follow orders. Doctors feared that "ladies" would be morally compromised by the sight of naked men and that they would faint or flirt, or both. In the event, more than 3,000 women served as nurses for the armies of both sides, many as unpaid volunteers.

There were precedents for women serving as nurses in a time of war: Florence Nightingale, a British nurse in the Crimean War in 1856, had become famous as the "Lady with the Lamp"; Jamaican native Mary Seacole also served in the Crimea and wrote a bestseller about her work there. In the United States so many women wanted to help in the war that nursing seemed to be the logical choice.

Dorothea Dix

On April 20, 1861, President Abraham Lincoln appointed a well-known reformer, Dorothea Dix, as superintendent of army nurses. Dix, who had spent years working with the mentally ill, headed the first official women's nursing group in the U.S. Army

Desensitization

The process of becoming immune to distress caused by witnessing terrible injuries, pain, or death.

Curriculum Context

If there were precedents for women being involved in war nursing, why might there have been so much reluctance for the same to happen in America, particularly in the South?

Curriculum Context

Students who are asked to describe the contribution of significant individuals to the war might consider using Dix as an example of a highly influential woman.

Medical Department. Dix did not want the "wrong" type of woman serving as a nurse: she would not hire anyone who was under 30 or pretty. She was not, she explained, running a marriage bureau. However, Dix's restrictions on who could serve did not last long. Union defeat at the first major battle of the war, the First Battle of Bull Run (Manassas), flooded Washington, D.C., with casualties in July 1861. Hospitals for the wounded were so short-handed that Dix began to accept anyone willing to volunteer.

In addition to the women Dix recruited, about 600 trained nursing nuns were supplied by religious orders. The U.S. Sanitary Commission, which was set up in June 1861 to provide care for sick and injured soldiers, supplied volunteer nurses from all over the North. In addition, women in towns near battle sites opened their homes as hospitals and spent time caring for the wounded, who slept on their floors or in their barns.

Hospital stewards

Nurses' duties varied with their experience and their proximity to battle. In battle and in camps nursing duties fell to hospital stewards. They combined the duties of orderly, nurse, and sometimes cook, depending on the needs of their regimental surgeon.

An army hospital in Beaufort, South Carolina, in 1864. Wounded soldiers who reached a general hospital like this had a better chance of survival, although there remained an ever-present danger of infection and disease, or gangrene in injured limbs.

Hospital stewards served as triage (sorting) nurses, prioritizing the wounded for medical attention; as ambulance transporters, moving wounded men into ambulances so they could be moved to the hospitals; and as record-keepers, keeping track of patients. Hospital stewards would also dispense medicines, assist during surgery in the field, and care for soldiers who recuperated in a regimental camp or hospital rather than being sent to a general hospital.

Women's duties

Women nurses spent most of their time in general hospitals established by the various armies. They were usually in major towns and cities near the battles and were for the long-term recuperation of wounded soldiers. Women had the same duties as male nurses, assisting in surgery, distributing medications, cleaning wounds, and changing dressings. Women nurses also bathed patients, fed men unable to feed themselves, gave them drink, read to them, and wrote their letters.

One of the most famous nurses on the Union side was Clara Barton, the "Angel of the Battlefield" for her heroic actions at Antietam and other battles. A 40-year-old clerk in the Patent Office when war broke out, she worked without pay, taking supplies to battlefields, searching for missing and wounded soldiers, and nursing on the battlefield. While she was holding a wounded soldier's head up so that he could drink water after the Battle of Antietam (Sharpsburg) in 1862, a Confederate bullet went through her dress, killing the soldier. Such a close call did not stop her. She continued to move supplies to the Union armies until 1864, when she was appointed superintendent of "diet and nursing" at a hospital for the X Corps, Army of the James. Susie King Taylor, a former slave from Savannah, Georgia, helped the Union cause as a nurse with an African American regiment in the Union army. She escaped slavery by boarding a Union vessel in 1862.

Triage
The process of sorting the wounded for priority of care: those whose lives could not be saved, those who needed immediate treatment, and those whose treatment was not so urgent.

Recuperation
Recovering one's former health, usually through an extended period of rest.

In the North there was a tradition of reform efforts by women's volunteer groups from which nurses could be drawn to make a nursing corps. In the South such organizations did not exist. Southern women helped the cause as best they could; but largely because the South was so rural, there was no tradition of women's reform organizations, and few resources. At the start of the war, instead of having an army department of nurses, the Confederate government asked individuals to open their houses to wounded soldiers.

Born a slave in 1848, Susie King Taylor was only 14 when she escaped with her uncle's family to the Union side in 1862. She joined the 1st South Carolina Volunteers, working first as a laundress and later as a nurse. In 1902 she wrote her Civil War memoirs.

Sally Tompkins

Sally Tompkins of Richmond, Virginia, persuaded a friend to offer his house as a hospital. Robertson Hospital opened in August 1861, and Tompkins was commissioned a captain in the cavalry by the Confederate government to run it, making her the only woman in the Confederacy with an army officer's commission. She spent her fortune supplying and staffing the hospital, which remained open throughout the war. Tompkins was unusual; most Southern nurses simply responded to the immediate calamity of battles in their home towns. Since so many Southerners lived on farms and most men were gone, it was difficult for Southern women to leave their farms to participate in the war effort. However, notable Southern nurses included Phoebe Yates Pember of Richmond, who helped run the Chimborazo Hospital in Richmond, and Kate Cumming.

The rigors of nursing

Nursing demanded both desensitization and physical strength. The medical treatments were often grisly, as were the wounds nurses saw. Limbs were amputated at the height of battle or later in hospitals, where gangrene set in and infection crept into the wounds. Soldiers lay on the field with various body parts blown off and had to be moved or treated amid the carnage.

Vivandières

In addition to the women who served as nurses in hospitals and with the army, another group of women performed nursing duties: the vivandières. Named for their French counterparts who served the French army in the days of Napoleon, vivandières were attached to specific army units, North and South. They wore trousers with a knee-length skirt over them, and jackets decorated with unit insignia. Known as "daughters of the regiment" they served, they worked as triage nurses, offering water or medicinal whiskey to wounded soldiers on the field.

In 1862 the poet Walt Whitman (1819–1892) traveled to a military hospital in Virginia to visit his brother George, wounded at the Battle of Fredericksburg. The traumatic experience led Whitman to volunteer as a nurse caring for wounded soldiers in Washington, D.C.

Experience of suffering

Although anesthesia had been developed by the 1840s, there might not be time to wait for it to take effect when lots of wounded appeared for treatment. In the South, as the blockade grew tighter, little anesthesia beyond whiskey could be had. Men would bite on a cloth to avoid biting through their tongues or screaming from the pain during an operation. The smells in hospitals set up in schools and private homes were awful. Nurses described wading through pools of blood, flies that were always present, having to lift men who weighed far more than they did. One nurse, Sarah Hussey, invented and patented a hospital table that provided a head and foot rest, with a sling to elevate limbs, to make it easier to care for patients.

On the home front wounded soldiers returning home also needed nursing. Women sometimes spent years nursing returning veterans back to health. Because of this, and because of the nursing work women did throughout the war, the profession of nursing came eventually to be seen as respectable "women's work."

Anesthesia
A drug that acts as a pain killer by deadening the senses or causing a temporary loss of consciousness.

Curriculum Context
Hussey's invention is a very unusual example of the role of technological innovation in the war.

Pacifism

When the Union and the Confederacy began to draft men into the armies, many pacifists came under severe pressure for their unwillingness to fight. In the Union the draft law was revised to offer the option of noncombatant duties.

Almost all those who refused military service in the Civil War were motivated by religious convictions. Pacifist religious groups had been influential in American society since colonial times. Pennsylvania was founded in 1674 as a refuge for the Society of Friends, or Quakers—a Christian group opposed to all war. In 1860 the Quakers had more than 200,000 members in the United States, mostly in the North. Other groups who opposed the war on religious grounds included the Mennonites, the Church of the Brethren, and utopian Christian communities such as the Shakers, the Oneida Community, and Adin Ballou's Hopedale. The major peace organization of the time was the American Peace Society (APS).

The Civil War created moral problems for pacifists, most of whom opposed slavery and hoped the conflict would lead to emancipation. Many secular pacifists either supported the conflict or remained silent. Indeed, the APS did not condemn the war. The abolitionist and pacifist Elihu Burritt (1810–1879) was a notable exception who advocated a program of compensated emancipation as an alternative to war.

Pacifists and the draft

Before the war each state required men to serve in the militia, but most provided alternatives for religious objectors. During the war a military draft was introduced in the Union and the Confederacy. Quaker and Shaker leaders sought exemption but it was refused, and most cases were dealt with individually.

Hopedale
A utopian community founded by Adin Ballou in Illinois in 1842 based on "practical Christianity."

Compensated emancipation
An alternative to the abolition of slavery under which slaveowners would be paid for the slaves they released.

In March 1863 the first Union draft law provided exemption for those willing to hire a substitute or pay a $300 fee. Many pacifists considered either alternative a contribution to the bloodshed. Some did pay the fee, and others fought—143 Quakers enlisted as Union soldiers. A revised draft law in February 1864 made provision for religious objectors. They could perform noncombatant service, usually in hospitals or assisting the freedmen, but few such placements were permitted. Objectors on both sides who were drafted and refused to obey orders were harshly treated. Pacifists were beaten or sentenced to military prison terms. Both Lincoln and Stanton were sympathetic to religious pacifists. When courts-martial were brought to their attention, they often intervened.

Freedmen
Slaves who had been emancipated during the war.

Confederate pacifists

Pacifists in the Confederacy faced harsher treatment due to shortages of men. The Confederate draft law of April 1862 made no provision for pacifists, but revised legislation in October 1862 exempted Quakers if they hired a substitute or paid an exemption fee of $500. Few could afford this. Southern objectors sometimes evaded service by hiding out or running to a Northern state. Some were court-martialed, beaten, or marched to the scene of battle. Men with strong convictions could not be forced into combat. General "Stonewall" Jackson suggested paroling them to farms where they would be more useful. Sidney S. Baxter, an official in the War Department, intervened on behalf of many objectors. Pacifists added to the tradition of nonviolence and started a debate that led the Union to offer the option of noncombatant service.

Illustration from the score of a Quaker song published in 1863 called "A Quaker Letter to Lincoln." Quakers sought to persuade Confederate and Union leaders to exempt pacifists from bearing arms.

Payment and Pensions

The promise of regular pay both attracted men to enlist and kept them in the service. After the Civil War the federal government and many states awarded pensions to veterans for battle wounds or simply for honorable service.

Curriculum Context

How soldiers were paid is an interesting topic for students learning about soldier life.

The Union and Confederate armies used similar pay systems and rates. Wages for enlisted soldiers in both armies were low, but increased as rank rose from private to sergeant. Privates in the Confederate army earned $11 per month until June 1864, when their wages increased to $18. Given the rampant inflation in the Confederacy this amount was essentially worthless. Problems in the Confederate administrative system meant the Southern soldiers were paid very irregularly. When the Confederacy was unable to provide its growing army with proper uniforms in the early months of the war, soldiers received a clothing allowance and purchased their own equipment. As the war went on, this provision became unnecessary.

Union army pay

Private soldiers in the Union army, earning $13 per month, also received a pay rise in 1864 and could expect a somewhat more regular schedule of payment. When African Americans were recruited into the Union army, privates received pay of only $10 per month, a decision that provoked great anger and resentment among soldiers in the black regiments. In addition, they did not receive the white soldier's $3 per month clothing supplement. After considerable protest, the Union government finally equalized wages for black and white soldiers in June 1864. However, the pay rise was only backdated to January 1, 1864, and applied only to African American troops who could prove their status as free men before the war. This discrimination denied thousands of black soldiers their rightful wages.

Curriculum Context

Students looking for examples of different groups of society during the war might consider comparing the experiences of white and African American soldiers in the Union army.

Officers' pay

Officers in both armies earned more money than enlisted men and were paid at different rates according to their branch or specialty. Union engineer and ordnance (military equipment and supplies) officers earned slightly more than their counterparts in the infantry, cavalry, and artillery. A second lieutenant of infantry earned $45 per month, while a colonel earned $95. All officers received additional "camp pay" to pay for uniforms, equipment, and living expenses. Union navy officers were paid yearly rather than monthly and had differing rates of pay depending on specialty.

In the Confederate army, cavalry and engineering officers earned more money than artillery and infantry officers. Lieutenants of cavalry earned $100 per month, a much higher wage than their Union counterparts, because Confederate officers had to buy and provide for their own horses.

Bounties

In addition to regular military pay thousands of Civil War soldiers earned money from another source: government, state, and local bounties, which were one-time payments to reward enlistment. Bounty payments were generous: as much as $600, equivalent to about five years' pay for a private. Thousands of men enlisted early in the war without resort to bounties; but as casualties mounted, it became harder to find men to enlist.

Although both the Union and Confederacy brought in government bounties early in the war, the introduction of the draft significantly changed the bounty system. The Confederacy passed its conscription act in 1862 and the Union in 1863. The draft acts gave individual states a quota of soldiers to enlist. State and local governments began to offer bounties to men who volunteered and avoided the shame of conscription.

Curriculum Context

Why might it have been necessary to pay such high bounties to get recruits to enlist?

Quota

A number of troops that each state had to contribute to the national army.

Desert

To abandon one's military service without permission.

Curriculum Context

The growth of state pension provision can be seen as one of the long-lasting social changes introduced by the Civil War.

Widespread offers of bounties caused resentment among soldiers who had enlisted before bounties were offered, and they encouraged "bounty jumping." This was a method whereby a recruit could obtain several bounties. The "bounty jumper" received a bounty for enlisting, then promptly deserted and reenlisted somewhere else for new bounties.

Military pensions

The U.S. military pension system came into existence after the American Revolution (1776–1783), when the new government began awarding pensions to soldiers wounded during active service or to impoverished widows. The Civil War resulted in unprecedented spending on pensions. At first pensions were offered only to those Union soldiers disabled by combat wounds, with the amount of pension offered depending on military rank and level of disability. The 1890 Dependent Pension Act made a significant change in the system. As a result of extensive lobbying by the Grand Army of the Republic (the main Union veterans' organization), the federal government extended pension benefits to anyone who served the Union honorably in the war and was later disabled while doing manual labor.

Confederate Pensions

Postwar attempts by Southern congressmen to extend pension benefits to Confederate veterans met with strong resistance. Much of this resistance came from well-off former Confederate soldiers, who saw any federal assistance as an insult to their service in the war. While poorer Southerners had no such qualms, Confederate veterans never became eligible for federal pensions. Into this gap stepped Southern state governments, which by the 1880s began to offer pensions as well as other benefits, such as veterans' retirement homes and artificial limbs. Provisions and payments varied from state to state, but Southern state pensions were different from federal pensions: They made no allowance for wartime rank, only for percentage of disability. Of all former Confederate states, Georgia and Alabama spent the most on pensions.

Photography

The Civil War was the first American war to be captured by the new technology, photography. For the first time people could see photographs of the dead on the battlefield, which dramatically brought home the brutality of war.

In 1861, photography was barely 20 years old. It had developed from early daguerreotype processes, which had been in use since 1839, and sitting for a photographic portrait had become very popular. Until 1880 the wet-plate method—for which a studio darkroom was essential—continued to be the standard method for developing a photographic negative. War photographers had to take a portable darkroom with them. The most famous traveling darkroom of the Civil War was Mathew Brady's "Whatsit," the nickname of his tarpaulin-covered, mule-drawn wagon.

Darkroom
A room in which film is developed without being exposed to daylight, which spoils the images.

Battle scenes
During the war many itinerant photographers, working for themselves, plied their trade in the camps. The war was also covered by the major photography firms, such as M.B. Brady, Alexander Gardner (Brady's former employee), E. & H.T. Anthony, and George S. Cook. Battle scenes could only be photographed after the fighting had finished, because it was too dangerous for a photographer to work while bullets and cannon balls flew around. The large box camera, mounted on a tall tripod, made photographers too conspicuous. As a result, battlefield photographs showed the aftermath of conflict: corpses strewn across the ground, dead horses, destroyed buildings, and devastated countryside. Most images were taken with a twin-lens stereoscopic camera and were called stereographs. The two images taken by the camera were then printed together. The result, when seen through a viewer, appeared three-dimensional.

Itinerant
Someone who moves around with no fixed base.

Curriculum Context
Some photographers are known to have moved corpses around to "improve" their photographs: does that make their images less valuable?

Curriculum Context

Most of these photographs now belong to the Library of Congress or the National Archives.

It is estimated that around 5,000 photographs of battle scenes, war equipment, and camp life were taken. The images were always in black and white—color photography was not invented until 1869.

Photographic portraits

Since it was difficult to photograph battles, most army camp photographers concentrated on portrait photography. At least 90 percent of all Civil War photographs were portraits. Photographers followed an army, and wherever it set up camp, they set up their temporary studio. Portrait photographers charged $1 per image: business was brisk, and photographers made good money. During the war 300 photographers were officially accredited by the Union military authorities, but historians think many more worked on the battlefields. Another 100 photographers worked in the South. Some estimates suggest that some 1,500 photographers took pictures for the press, the public, or the military. However, some battles went unphotographed, while others, such as Gettysburg, were covered by many photographers.

The South produced the first war photographers; but as supplies of chemicals ran out, it became difficult for them to print the images they took. As a result, the war on the Southern side is less well documented.

Mathew Brady's photographic gallery in New York in January 1861. Before the Civil War Brady specialized in portrait photography, and during the war his pictures focused on the glorious aspect of war. Because it was not technologically possible to print photographs in newspapers, photographic galleries were important in showing images of war to the public.

Portrait Gallery

n 1862 an account in the magazine *Scientific American* described the popularity in the army of the traveling photographic studios:

"One of the institutions of our army is the traveling portrait gallery. A camp is hardly pitched before one of the omnipresent artists in collodion and amber-varnish draws up in his two-horse wagon, pitches his canvas gallery, and unpacks his chemicals. . . . Their tents are thronged from morning to night. . . . [The Bergstresser brothers] have followed the army for more than a year, and taken, the Lord only knows how many thousand portraits."

Famous photographers

The Union produced the Civil War's most famous photographer, Mathew Brady, who was eager to be known as the chief war photographer. A successful portrait photographer, Brady chose to concentrate on the glories of war. His pictures show a proud and strong army. Soldiers strike a commanding pose while leaning on a flag post, often with one knee bent as they look straight at the camera. Brady photographed troops in the field, in camp, on board ships, and against the walls of their fort. Very few of Brady's photographs capture the devastation of war, although he was present at several major campaigns, including the first Battle of Bull Run, Antietam, and Gettysburg.

Captain Andrew Joseph Russell was a soldier and the only photographer with official status, meaning he was able to charge the War Department for his work. He was instructed to make a photographic record of all the engineering problems caused by the fighting.

Etchings and exhibitions

Photographs could not be reproduced in newspapers during the Civil War because no one had yet invented a way of putting a photograph directly onto a printing plate. That did not happen until 1880. Instead, newspaper readers relied on etchings of battle scenes,

Etching
A method of printing by engraving lines in a metal plate, which is then inked to produce an image on a piece of paper.

"Harvest of Death," taken by Timothy O'Sullivan, shows slain soldiers littering the field after the Battle of Gettysburg in July 1863.

which were better able to capture rapid action. It took artists as long as two weeks to produce an etching to accompany a story. Once photographs could be printed, the news appeared in print much quicker. People visited exhibitions of war photographs held in galleries in New York and other Union cities to see images of war and photographic portraits of generals with familiar names but whose appearance was only known from etchings and newspaper portraits.

As the war ended, the public's appetite for images of the conflict died away. It was only in 1872 that the War Department paid Brady $25,000 for his collection of negatives, realizing the historical importance of a photographic archive for the nation.

Curriculum Context

Why might it be important for the nation to own an archive of such a destructive conflict?

Harvest of Death

Two of Mathew Brady's employees, Alexander Gardner (1821–1882) and Timothy O'Sullivan (1840–1882), captured the stark brutality of the war. Their photographs of unburied corpses lying on a devastated battlefield are some of the most enduring images of the Civil War. In his *Photographic Sketchbook of the War* (1866) Gardner published 100 photographs, of which 75 show battlefields and landscapes, 15 camp life, and fewer than 10 are portraits. O'Sullivan's most famous photograph, "Harvest of Death," was taken after the battle at Gettysburg. It shows corpses strewn across the battlefield with the pockets of their jackets turned out and their boots stolen. On the far horizon are two figures, one on a horse, the only living things amid a field of death.

Propaganda

The shaping of public opinion is crucial in wartime, yet neither the Lincoln nor the Davis administration systematically produced propaganda to convince their own populations of the justness of their cause.

The war was fought mainly on Confederate soil. The Confederacy could only maintain the war effort with the support of its population, and it could not draw on the traditions of loyalty and patriotism that were open to the Unionists. Yet, despite the obvious need to enlist public opinion in support of the Confederacy, President Jefferson Davis seems to have given little attention to propaganda. He did undertake several speaking tours in various parts of the Confederacy in 1863 and 1864, and proclaimed days of fasting and prayer from time to time, but such activities were hardly a sustained propaganda campaign.

Unofficial propaganda in the South was barely more effective. The press was subject to very little regulation or censorship, to the extent that military information useful to the enemy often appeared in the columns of Southern newspapers. Some newspapermen did give the Davis administration steady support, but they were outnumbered by critics who wrote with little restraint.

The church proved a more successful conduit for unofficial propaganda in the South. Southern society was deeply religious, and religion was a key factor in stirring and maintaining enthusiasm for the war. The clergy offered solace to the bereaved and injured, while deserters and speculators were condemned as both offensive to God and detrimental to the war effort. Confederate victories were seen to confirm Southerners' status as God's chosen people, while defeats were accepted as penance for their sins.

Curriculum Context

Propaganda can be classed as either "white"—propaganda that promotes the side that produces it—or "black" propaganda, which sets out to criticize the enemy.

Speculators

Businessmen who invest in commodities in the hopes that shortages or other circumstances will allow them to make big profits in the future.

The Rhetoric of Abraham Lincoln

Although Abraham Lincoln did not engage in a concerted domestic propaganda program, his speeches and public utterances played an important role in rallying Union opinion to the cause. They were often published and distributed by nonofficial propaganda organizations such as the Union Leagues.

Two of the most effective examples of Lincoln's rhetoric were the Gettysburg Address and the public letters on civil liberties that the president issued following the arrest of the anti-war Democrat leader Clement L. Vallandigham in 1863. Lincoln famously asked those who were critical of Vallandigham's arrest, "Must I shoot a simple-minded soldier boy who deserts, while I must not touch a hair of a wily agitator who induces him to desert?" On the curtailment of civil liberties in wartime he asserted that he no more believed it would establish precedents fatal to liberty in peacetime "than I am able to believe that a man could contract so strong an appetite for emetics during temporary illness, as to persist in feeding upon them through the remainder of his healthful life."

Propaganda in the North

In the Union propaganda activities were scarcely better organized. There was no official program aimed at maintaining enthusiasm for the conflict. President Abraham Lincoln's finely crafted speeches were important in rallying public opinion to the Union cause, but Lincoln himself showed little interest in the potential of propaganda.

Most Union propaganda was produced by nonofficial organizations, notably the Union Leagues, which were maintained by middle-class enthusiasts. The first such league was formed in Philadelphia in 1862. Its founders were primarily Republicans, but they placed emphasis more on support for the war and the Union than for the Lincoln administration itself.

Within a year the league movement had spread over 18 Northern states and even begun to make an appearance among Unionists in the South. The leagues operated as rallying points for citizen support of the Union cause, raising money for relief of the troops, promoting enlistment in the army, and distributing leaflets designed to rally support for the war effort. The Loyal Publication Society, established by the Union League of New York, raised nearly $30,000 during the three years of its existence and published 900,000 copies of 90 different pamphlets. They were distributed to league organizations across the Union and to soldiers serving at the front.

As in the South, the conflict was staunchly supported from the pulpit, but disagreements over emancipation made the notion of a holy war more difficult to countenance. Likewise, there was little regulation of the press by the Lincoln administration. Newspapers and periodicals flourished in the Union: most were fiercely partisan and packed as much with rumor and speculation as with concrete news of the conflict. They expressed a spectrum of opinion both sympathetic to and critical of the administration.

Propaganda in Europe
Although the administrations of North and South paid little attention to propaganda within their own borders, the importance of the battle for opinion in Europe (especially Britain and France) was clear to all. From the beginning of the conflict European intervention was seen as a key factor that could win or lose the war. Moreover, it was understood that the best means of procuring the support of the British and French was not through diplomatic missions but by mobilizing the European clergy and press to present a "correct" understanding of the conflict. The prime minister of Britain, Lord Palmerston, had built his political reputation on a fiercely independent foreign policy. He was unlikely to risk being seen to act at the bidding of a foreign delegation, but he might be prepared to commit his country to supporting one side or the other if domestic opinion demanded it and so propaganda initiatives were thought important.

Diplomatic

Concerning negotiations and relations between different countries.

Propaganda initiatives

Both the Confederacy and the Union accompanied their diplomatic overtures to Europe with propaganda initiatives. The Lincoln administration dispatched a steady stream of visitors to Europe during the course of the war, many especially selected to appeal to European pressure groups or interests. Union representatives included John Hughes, the Catholic archbishop of New York, whose mission was to gain the support of the papacy and the Catholic rulers of continental Europe; Bishop McIlvaine of the Protestant Episcopal Church, who was to lobby the English clergy; and the New York political operator Thurlow Weed, who was to try to promote the Union cause among

John Hughes (1797–1864), the first Catholic archbishop of New York, who was sent on a diplomatic mission to Europe by President Abraham Lincoln to try to enlist the support of the pope and the European Catholic rulers for the Union cause.

European journalists. European opinion was wooed with leaflets extolling the benefits to immigrants of the Homestead Act. Despite Lincoln's domestic reluctance to make the war an antislavery crusade, the issue was a trump card in European countries, which had abolished slavery within their own colonies decades previously. Union representatives helped organize public meetings in Britain, which passed resolutions endorsing emancipation.

Curriculum Context

When judging the impact of Lincoln's Emancipation Proclamation, students should remember to consider its effect on public opinion outside North America.

Cotton diplomacy

The South used cotton to try to pressure countries such as Britain and France to support the Confederacy. By starving the European countries of raw cotton, on which they were heavily dependent, it was hoped the British and French would be induced to enter the war on the Confederate side. More subtle efforts were also made to win over European public opinion. They were masterminded by the chief Confederate propaganda agent, Henry Hotze. English writers were employed to publicize the Confederate cause in newspapers and periodicals. Favorable books and pamphlets were printed and freely distributed to politicians and others in positions of influence. Most importantly, Hotze was responsible for *The Index*, a special newspaper published in London to present Southern views. Although *The Index* itself never achieved wide circulation, it provided copy for many other papers in Britain and elsewhere. Thus its message reached large audiences.

Periodical

A publication such as a magazine that is published regularly but with a set interval between each issue.

Public Opinion

There were many ways to gauge public opinion between elections. Newspapers and popular songs reflected the public mood, voluntary organizations showed support for the war effort, while discontent burst out in riots and desertions.

Throughout the war there were many observers recording the public reaction to events. In March 1861, after secession but before the attack on Fort Sumter, William Howard Russell, the distinguished war correspondent for *The Times* newspaper of London, arrived in New York to report on the crisis for his readers in Britain. To his astonishment, he found that New Yorkers were going about their business as though nothing much was afoot. Russell could see no signs of preparations for war. He was amazed to find that even among elite New York society, there was "not the smallest evidence of uneasiness on account of circumstances which, to the eye of a stranger, betokened an awful crisis, if not the dissolution of society itself." He also noted that these same upper-class New Yorkers sneered at their newly elected president, Abraham Lincoln. Many mocked his popular nickname: "the Rail Splitter," which alluded to the laboring work Lincoln had done as a young man from a poor background.

Mood in the South

Russell then headed off to the South to get a feel for the mood there. On April 12–13 Confederate forces shelled Fort Sumter into submission; the war had officially begun, although there had as yet been no serious battle. Wherever he went, Russell found the populace in festive mood, with everyone excited and bubbling over with anticipation at the coming conflict—and utterly confident of its outcome, convinced it would be over in a matter of months. It

Curriculum Context

How would it have been possible for Northerners to be so oblivious to the coming of war?

Curriculum Context

What grounds would Southerners have had in spring 1861 to imagine that they would win victory in a few months?

was as though the outbreak of hostilities had provided a release for all the pent-up emotion created by the long national crisis. If Russell had been back in New York at that moment—or in any other big Northern city—he would have witnessed similar scenes of jubilation. War fever was in the air. A quarter of New York's 800,000 population turned out for a rally in Union Square on April 20, while recruits flocked to the Union colors in response to the president's call—immediately after the attack on Fort Sumter—for 75,000 volunteers.

When Russell did return to New York a few months later, it was to find the city caught up in the war, with recruiting posters on the walls and men in uniform on the streets.

A people's war
Right from the beginning there were concerted efforts to make the war to preserve the Union a people's war. In New York alone a whole raft of soldiers' aid and relief

Curriculum Context

Do you think that the popular reaction to the outbreak of war would have been different if people knew how long the conflict would last?

The United States Sanitary Commission

In April 1861 a group of prominent New York women met to discuss how they could best coordinate their various charitable activities to help the war effort. This resulted in the formation of the United States Sanitary Commission.

The Sanitary Commission's main effort went into supplying food, clothing, and bandages for the wounded on the battlefield and the sick and wounded in army camps. It also monitored army hospitals and medical treatment, and provided relief for soldiers who had fallen on hard times and for their families. As the war went on, the Sanitary Commission became extremely high profile, both for its relief activities and for its spectacular success in raising funds. In January 1863 the women of Lowell, Massachusetts, held a Sanitary Fair that raised nearly $5,000. This was followed by a fair in Chicago in October, which raised the then enormous sum of nearly $80,000. In keeping with the spirit of the event, President Lincoln donated his original manuscript of the Emancipation Proclamation, with an accompanying letter saying, a little ruefully perhaps, that "I had some desire to retain the paper, but if it shall contribute to the relief and comfort of the soldiers, that will be better."

A sheet-music cover showing a woman representing Liberty holding the Stars and Stripes. The Union flag became the focus of patriotism for the Northern states during the Civil War.

HAIL! GLORIOUS BANNER OF OUR LAND.

Curriculum Context

Some curricula might ask students to describe ways in which women were able to make a contribution to the progress of the war.

societies sprang into existence. Churches and schools threw themselves into making and collecting useful things for the troops. Voluntary efforts of this type were quickly brought under the huge umbrella of the United States Sanitary Commission, which enabled Northern women especially to make a really significant contribution to the lives of the troops at the front. In its tireless activities to promote the soldiers' welfare the Sanitary Commission was also an effective agency for drumming up support for the war itself.

Just as the Sanitary Commission both reflected and influenced public opinion, so too did other opinion-forming institutions in the Union. Church leaders preached sermons extolling patriotism and reviling slavery, and these sermons were often reprinted and widely distributed. In 1863 the Loyal Publications

Society was set up in New York for the express purpose of pouring out pro-Union material for the reading public. In Boston the North East Loyal Publications Society went about the same task in a different way. It gathered up little snippets of pro-Union—or anti-Confederate—comment and gossip from any source it could find and then sent it out to the many small-town newspapers. Hardworking editors were grateful to receive free copy, and readers to receive confirmation of their convictions.

Wavering support

Support for the war among the Northern public remained generally steady, with two significant dips. The first reflected disillusionment with General George B. McClellan's ineffectual Peninsular Campaign in the summer of 1862. It was only with the Union army's determined showing at the Battle of Antietam (Sharpsburg) in September 1862 that support returned to its previous levels.

Two years later, in the summer of 1864, there was again real war-weariness in the North. General William T. Sherman was camped outside Atlanta but seemingly unable to take that Southern stronghold, while General Ulysses S. Grant in Virginia could not land a knockout blow on Confederate General Robert E. Lee. Instead of the patriotic war songs of earlier years, the sheet-music bestseller now was "When This Cruel War Is Over."

Many influential voices in his own party told Lincoln that he should revoke the Emancipation Proclamation and attempt a peace settlement that would leave Southern slavery in place. Although the president refused to consider such a step, he fully expected to lose his bid for reelection in November. He told an army officer, "I am going to be beaten, and unless some great change takes place, badly beaten." However, great changes did take place—Atlanta fell

Curriculum Context

You may be asked to describe the effect of military success or failure on public opinion in the North and South.

to Sherman in early September, and Grant finally pinned down Lee's army in Petersburg and Richmond. Lincoln was safely reelected in November, and opinion in the North now supported his war aims to the end.

Opinion in the South

Public opinion among whites in the Confederacy remained solidly behind the fight for Southern independence throughout the war, apart from southern Unionists, who had never supported it. Unlike the situation in the North, where abandoning the war was at least an option, Southerners saw the Civil War as a fight for survival—the war for Southern independence, as it was often called. Success on the battlefield in the early years of the war confirmed people's confidence in Southern military prowess. When the tide finally turned against the exhausted Confederate armies, there was little inclination to rethink the rights and wrongs of the whole situation. Despite alarming levels of desertion during the grim winter months of early 1865, those at the front as well as those at home bore their defeat with stoicism and a fair measure of defiance.

Curriculum Context

What might the Confederacy have expected if it had surrendered earlier in the war?

Stoicism

An ability to remain indifferent to suffering and pain.

Turning Slaves into Soldiers

Toward the end of the war, when they were staring defeat in the face, Southern politicians and opinion-makers—with President Jefferson Davis in the lead—launched into a heated debate as to whether it might be possible to impress slaves into the Confederate army. Davis favored the move as being necessary to save the Confederacy. But what, demanded his critics, would that do to the institution of slavery, which was what the Confederacy had been created to defend? Surely it would be impossible to arm slaves and expect them to fight for the Confederate cause without granting or promising them freedom?

The impassioned debate brought back to the surface the whole tangle of twisted logic that had been used a generation earlier in defense of slavery. The spectacle reduced some Southerners to hollow laughter. As one jaded newspaper editor put it, "Our Southern people have not gotten over the vicious habit of not believing what they don't wish to believe."

Recruitment

The Civil War was the nation's first experience of a war that involved mass armies of hundreds of thousands of men. Before such vast forces could be trained or take to the battlefield, they had first to be recruited.

The recruitment process was essentially the same for both the Union and the Confederacy: Each president issued a call for a number of volunteers, and each state was responsible for supplying a quota of recruits. State governors in turn contacted prominent local men in the cities and towns of their states—politicians, lawyers, businessmen—who then issued calls for volunteers in their districts. Early in the war these men themselves frequently became the commanders of volunteer regiments, units of approximately 1,000 men.

These prominent men often used other men of like stature to help them recruit in particular areas. Broadsides, or recruiting posters, were printed and distributed, advertising a time and place for volunteers to rally and sign up. Recruiting officers held meetings at a county seat or other prominent place and provided patriotic music and speeches to encourage men to enlist. During one such Confederate recruiting drive in eastern Tennessee, the recruiter paid for a brass band to march up and down the town's main street after dark, accompanied by torches and fireworks.

Recruiting process

The recruiting method of one regiment of the famous Union "Iron Brigade," the 19th Indiana Infantry, is a good example of the process. In April 1861, after the Confederate capture of Fort Sumter became public knowledge, volunteer companies sprang up all over the North. Indiana was no exception. As soon as the news reached Wayne County by telegraph, Solomon

Curriculum Context

Some of these prominent men proved less-than-able as military commanders; the standard of fighting improved as professional officers took command.

Curriculum Context

You might be asked to describe the process of recruiting soldiers for the conflict.

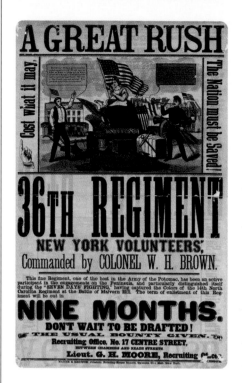

An 1863 recruitment poster for the 36th New York Infantry. Volunteers were offered a nine-month term of enlistment and "the usual bounty."

Meredith, the county clerk, called a meeting at the county courthouse, where he urged the assembled men to elect officers and organize military companies. In June Indiana Governor Oliver Morton issued a call for six regiments of infantry. He commissioned Meredith to raise one of them. Meredith spread the word by telegraph and newspaper that he would accept into his regiment companies formed by local captains. Within a day companies began arriving in Indianapolis, the state capital. Morton moved the first few companies that arrived to a "camp of instruction" for new units on the outskirts of the city. The tenth and final company arrived in camp on July 15.

Initial success

Initial recruiting drives in the North and South were easy and remarkably successful. Fueled by the desire to attain military glory and the mistaken belief the war would be short and relatively bloodless, thousands rushed to enlist in the infantry, cavalry, or artillery. President Abraham Lincoln's initial call for 75,000 volunteers to suppress the rebellion was filled within days, prompting the overconfident Union government to turn away thousands of disappointed recruits.

Recruiting in the Confederacy was equally successful, and regiments filled quickly. But the First Battle of Bull Run in July 1861 and the Battle of Shiloh in April 1862 ended hopes of a quick and bloodless struggle. In the aftermath of Bull Run the U.S. Congress authorized the president to call for up to 500,000 three-year volunteers, and hundreds of new volunteer regiments came into being. The Confederate Congress made a similar move in August, calling for 400,000 volunteers.

Bull Run

Northerners were so confident of victory in the first battle of the war that they went to Bull Run to watch: the spectators got caught up with the panicked retreat of the Union troops at the end of the day.

The next call for volunteers occurred in the North in July 1862, as the fortunes of the war in the East turned against the Union. Lincoln declared a military emergency and called for an additional 300,000 three-year volunteers. These troops served for the remainder of the war. Meanwhile, the enlistments of the men who volunteered in summer 1861 ran out during the 1864 Virginia campaign; many troops quit George G. Meade's Army of the Potomac as it tried to destroy Lee's army north of Richmond. In an attempt to keep veteran soldiers in the ranks, the Union army offered furloughs (leave) and "Veteran Volunteer" status to those who reenlisted. This kept enough veterans to maintain the progress of the campaign, but the Union army's effectiveness was compromised by the continual introduction of conscripts into the ranks.

Furlough

An extended period of leave from duty for a soldier or other service-man, for example to allow them to return home.

Conscription

The introduction of conscription created a second source of soldiers for both armies. The need became apparent in the Confederacy, when spring 1862 saw the expiration of the original one-year enlistments. The Confederacy introduced conscription in 1862, and the Union the following year, when the need for large numbers of soldiers began to outstrip the numbers of volunteers. The Confederate Congress passed the first of three conscription acts on April 16, 1862; the first national military draft in American history. All men already serving had to reenlist for the war's duration and all other white males, between 18 and 35, to enlist. Following the Confederacy, the Union passed the first of its six conscription acts in March 1863. The draft was as unpopular in the North as in the South.

Curriculum Context

The South's conscription act can be seen as a turning point in American history.

While conscription succeeded in filling the ranks of the armies, it raised doubts about the breakdown of civil liberties in wartime. It resulted in corruption and violence, while raising the status of the volunteer citizen-soldier in the American consciousness.

Curriculum Context

Many curricula ask students to consider the fate of civil liberties during the war.

Religion

Religion played an important role in everyday life in the 19th century. The United States was one of the most religiously active countries in the world in terms of church members and the influence that religion had in national politics.

Some four million adults in the United States were members of churches in the mid-19th century. Millions of children attended Sunday schools, which were often where they learned to read and write. Millions more adults attended religious services regularly without formally joining the membership. Most religious groups were Protestant, and those that were not were generally regarded with suspicion. Many Catholics and Jews suffered discrimination.

Curriculum Context

Catholicism was closely associated with recent groups of immigrants, such as Irish and Italians.

Most 19th-century Americans believed in a divine Providence, an all-powerful God who made the world, ruled it actively, allowed evil to exist, and produced good. Everything that happened did so for God's reasons and to fulfill his designs and plans for the world. They also believed in sin (separation from God) and salvation, which brought sinners back to God through the death and resurrection of Jesus Christ, the son of God. Life was short, death was certain and universal, and heaven, where there would be no more pain and no more sorrow, awaited all who believed in the saving power of Jesus Christ.

Second Great Awakening

Great Awakening

The First Great Awakening had lasted from abut 1725 to about 1750.

There had been a huge Protestant religious revival in the United States between 1820 and 1860, known as the Second Great Awakening. Evangelicals, who focused their preaching on Jesus, salvation, and the damnation of sinners, held meetings that could attract crowds of up to 25,000 people. The Second Great Awakening led to many Christians coming to see slavery as a sin. In the 1850s churches were split over this issue. Abolitionists called slavery a sin, while proslavers argued it was necessary to "civilize" and Christianize African "heathens." Other proslavers even said that African slaves had no souls that needed to be saved. Major churches such as the Presbyterian, Baptist, Episcopalian, and Methodist denominations were often internally divided over what position to take on slavery. In many churches the split took years to heal.

Most of the soldiers who went to war believed in a supreme Being, and the majority were Protestant Christians. Among the rest were Catholics, some Jews, and a very few atheists (atheism was referred to as "infidelity" and only really existed in Northern cities).

Laws throughout the country forbade conducting any business on a Sunday. At first, commanders tried to respect the rules of the Sabbath. Confederate General Robert E. Lee ordered only work essential to the safety, health, or comfort of the army be undertaken on Sunday. Union General George B. McClellan issued similar orders. However, war was unpredictable that could not always be postponed until Sunday was over.

Men of the 9th Massachusetts Infantry with their chaplain before a church service at Camp Cass, Virginia, in 1861. Chaplains in the Northern armies were paid, but most chaplains with the Confederate armies at the beginning of the war were unpaid.

No place for religion

Many soldiers' letters home commented on how the Sabbath was not respected. Not only were church services rare, but soldiers routinely ignored its moral lessons. Bad habits such as cursing, playing cards, gambling, and drinking—all sins according to many Protestant churches—were widespread. In the first year of the war men seemed determined to throw off any religious restraints, but later a religious revival took place. Both sides, after seeing so much death, coped by accepting God's will was at work, and it was divine Providence that had either kept them safe or taken them to heaven.

Army chaplains

Army chaplains held services for the troops, they also conducted funerals, provided private counseling, comforted the sick, gave out religious reading materials, and wrote letters home. Northern armies paid chaplains $145 a month from the outset; Southern armies began with volunteer chaplains, eventually paying them $80 a month. The chaplains occupied a unique place: As volunteers, they rode horses like officers, but were not provided with forage for them; they received no uniforms and, for much of the war, were issued only a private's rations. Some chaplains entered the ministry to avoid soldiering (although some fought alongside the troops); some were not even ordained ministers. Some chaplains worked with several regiments, preaching four or five times a day.

Christian volunteers

Missionaries who visited the camps and hospital also provided support. The U.S. Christian Commission, founded by the Young Men's Christian Association in 1861, had 5,000 volunteers who distributed literature, stamps, envelopes and stationery, and provided food, humanitarian aid, and comfort for the wounded on the battlefields and in the army hospitals.

Curriculum Context

There were a number of recorded instances where men's lives were saved when the Bible they carried in their chest pocket stopped a bullet.

Forage
Fodder for animals.

Sickness and Disease

Disease killed two-thirds of the men who died during the Civil War. Cramped, filthy living conditions in camp, bad weather, insects, and poor diet all contributed to the high incidence of sickness and disease among soldiers.

In the early 1860s European scientists such as Louis Pasteur in France, Robert Koch in Germany, and Joseph Lister in Britain were beginning to explore the role of bacteria in spreading infection. But for the soldiers there was not yet any widespread understanding of how bacteria thrive in unhygienic conditions and spread disease. This knowledge developed too late to prevent the medical disaster caused by the Civil War.

Bacteria
Microorganisms that spread disease.

Frequent illness

An estimated 400,000 of the 620,000 men who died during the war died from disease. Even more fell sick. In the first year there were 3,000 cases of sickness for every 1,000 Union soldiers, meaning a soldier got sick three times a year on average. The rate was higher for the Union's black troops. The Confederates, whose records were lost after the fall of Richmond in 1865, suffered just as badly, with each Southern soldier falling ill at least five times during his service.

Harewood Hospital in Washington, D.C., photographed during the war. The beds are covered with nets to protect the patients from insect bites, but soldiers had no such protection in camp. It was not known that mosquitoes transmitted malaria, and some 10,000 Union soldiers were killed by the disease.

Lack of medical checks

The problems began in 1861. In the rush to enlist men fewer than half the Union recruits were given medical checks. In spring 1862 the Union army found so many invalids in its ranks it dismissed 200,000 men who were too weak to serve. In the Confederacy there were no medical checks at all until 1862.

No immunity

The physical weakness of many recruits and lack of medical checks meant infectious diseases entered the training camps spreading rapidly to become epidemics. Recruits from isolated rural communities were worst affected because they had rarely been exposed to many sources of infection, and had not built up immunity. The first diseases were common ones, such as measles and chicken pox. For an adult without immunity they can be deadly. In 1861 three Confederate regiments from Mississippi lost 204 men through measles in three months.

Filthy conditions

The dirt and lack of hygiene in camp encouraged disease. An inspector from the U.S. Sanitary Commission, described one Union army camp as "littered with refuse, food and other rubbish, sometimes in an offensive state of decomposition; slops deposited in pits within the camp limits or thrown out of broadcast; heaps of manure and offal close to the camp." This was largely the fault of the military authorities, who gave little thought to how thousands of men could be housed together and kept clean and healthy. In the Union army men were supposed to wash their hands and faces daily, and bathe once a week, while latrines known as "sinks" were meant to be dug as an open trench away from the tents. But many soldiers did not wash so frequently, which encouraged vermin such as fleas and lice. Soldiers went to the bathroom in any convenient place,

Curriculum Context

Students describing soldier life in the Civil War should consider the constant threat from infectious diseases and why they were so prevalent.

Latrines

A communal toilet in a barracks or camp.

Diarrhea and Dysentery

Bowel disorders were rife among Civil War soldiers. Diarrhea was caused by poor diet and contaminated drinking water. The Union army reported that of 1,740,000 cases of diarrhea or dysentery (an infection of the intestine resulting in severe diarrhea characterized by blood in the stool), 58,000 soldiers died. At the Confederate Chimborazo Hospital in Richmond the death rate among diarrhea and dysentery patients was one in ten. Soldiers nicknamed diarrhea "the Tennessee Trots" or "Virginia Quickstep," but their lightheartedness could not conceal the seriousness of these illnesses. Nearly half of Union General Ulysses S. Grant's force besieging Vicksburg, Mississippi, in 1863 were incapacitated with diarrhea and dysentery. Cholera and typhoid, which are intestinal infections that cause severe diarrhea, also struck in camp.

turning camps into fields of excrement. This contaminated sources of drinking water, and spread diarrhea, dysentery, and typhoid. The dirt attracted flies, fleas, and lice, which spread germs.

Typhoid
A serious intestinal infection spread by bacteria in infected food or water.

Life on campaign

Poor diet worsened the soldiers' health. Hard marching and exposure weakened men living on rations of pickled beef or salt pork, hardtack biscuit, and coffee. The diet did not keep men strong enough to ward off sickness. Shortages of vegetables and fruit meant that many men developed scurvy, due to a lack of vitamin C. Confederates often had no decent uniforms, boots, or raincoats. By the end most Southern soldiers only had a thin blanket to keep them warm, so lung diseases such as pneumonia and bronchitis became common. In summer, men based along the rivers and swampy lowlands of the South caught fevers—"swamp wreck" or the "ague," which was malaria. Scientists did not yet know that mosquitoes transmitted the disease. Badly chosen campsites plagued with clouds of insects saw outbreaks of "the shakes" within days. The Union army reported more than a million cases of malaria. The cure was not known, so those with non-life-threatening cases had to live with it.

Hardtack
A staple food of the Civil War, hardtack was a hard biscuit made only of flour and water.

Sultana Disaster

On the night of April 27–28, 1865, the steamship *Sultana* exploded while sailing up the Mississippi River, killing an estimated 1,700 passengers. Most of the dead were Union soldiers returning home from Confederate prisoner-of-war camps.

During the second half of April 1865 a whirlwind of events swept the nation—Lincoln was murdered; and Confederate President Jefferson Davis went on the run. Amid all the drama and confusion, on the night of April 27–28 the steamship *Sultana* blew up on the Mississippi River just north of Memphis, Tennessee, with huge loss of life—the worst maritime disaster in U.S. history. The Sultana was licensed to carry 300 passengers. On this fateful voyage, however, it was packed with perhaps as many as 2,300 people, most of them released Union prisoners of war who had boarded at Vicksburg and were bound for Cairo, Illinois.

Nighttime explosion

At 2:00 A.M. on April 28, the grossly overcrowded vessel was laboring against a strong current, when one of its boilers exploded. The sound of the explosion was so loud it could be heard downriver in Memphis. Many of the returning soldiers, weakened by hunger and disease, were in poor shape. Hundreds were flung into the air and into the river, where many drowned, while hundreds more were trapped aboard and consumed in the fire that followed the explosion.

The actual death toll is not known because in the scramble to board the *Sultana* at Vicksburg no proper muster was made. The generally accepted figure is 1,700—more than died when the *Titanic* sank in 1912. However, while the *Titanic* disaster gripped the imagination of the world, the *Sultana* horror passed largely unnoticed in the aftermath of war.

Muster

To gather soldiers together in an assembly.

Supplies

The saying that "an army marches on its stomach" was certainly true during the Civil War. The armies of both sides also needed a range of supplies in addition to food to ensure that their soldiers were properly equipped and protected.

In order to supply hundreds of thousands of soldiers, both sides set up commissary departments to acquire, store, sell, and distribute supplies. The army officers responsible for supplies for each unit were called quartermasters. The prewar U.S. Army was fairly small, with just a few thousand frontier and garrison troops, and extensive supply systems were unnecessary. When the Union and Confederacy began to mobilize large armies in 1861, they had to create the systems from virtually nothing. The Union army had the benefit of a small U.S. Army Quartermaster Department, which had existed since 1812; but it was incapable of supplying the rapidly expanding army.

Curriculum Context

Keeping an army supplied was arguably as great a challenge as meeting the enemy on the battlefield.

Montgomery C. Meigs

On June 13, 1861, Montgomery C. Meigs became quartermaster general of the Union army, a position he held for the rest of the war. His first task was to supply the volunteers called up by President Lincoln. Lincoln relied on state governments to equip their soldiers but they lacked sufficient equipment so thousands of men reported for duty without proper uniforms or weapons. Cloth for uniforms was an early need and U.S. factories increased their production. By the time the armies took to the field for active campaigning, there was no shortage of uniforms for Union troops.

A Union commissary depot at Cedar Level, Virginia, during the Siege of Petersburg (June 1864–April 1865). Supply wagons can be seen next to the stores.

The Union Quartermaster Department

At the start of the war Union quartermaster officers in the armies and their subordinate units issued contracts for supplies. Quartermaster officers could also buy supplies on the open market. While this system was very flexible, it was also open to corruption and poor quality, since the government was not able to check for shoddy goods and dishonest contractors. To resolve these problems, Meigs centralized contracting and expanded the Quartermaster Department in Washington. He reorganized the department into nine divisions, one each responsible for animals, clothing, ocean and lake transportation, rail and river transportation, forage and fuel, barracks and hospitals, wagons, inspections, and finance. Each division chief issued contracts to suppliers in their areas and then inspected all goods and services before they reached the armies.

The Union army had the benefit of a well-run Quartermaster Department, plentiful materials, and an extensive network of railroads to distribute supplies and depots to store goods. Vast quantities of food, uniforms, knapsacks, tents, blankets, weapons, ammunition, and other equipment, such as horses, wagons, and pontoon bridges, flowed to the men in the field, ensuring that the Union army was one of the best supplied in military history.

Curriculum Context

To what extent do you think that the Union's superior supplies reflect the Union's economic and industrial superiority?

Confederate supplies

The first Confederate quartermaster general, Abraham C. Myers, set up a system based on the Union model, but had a more difficult task than the Union. The first volunteers were adequately clothed for warm weather, but wool for winter clothing was in short supply. Myers looked overseas, particularly to England, for supplies but this source was reduced by the Union blockade. Many Southern manufacturing facilities were in areas that fell to Union forces early, such as Nashville, Tennessee, and New Orleans, Louisiana.

Myers discovered, as Meigs had, that his bureau suffered from corruption and poor quality supplies, so he, too, reorganized in early 1863. The Confederacy was split into 11 purchasing districts, giving his staff greater control. Local supply officers often relied on the impressment of livestock and foodstuffs, often with little or no compensation to owners. This, combined with increasing shortages on the home front, fed growing Southern discontent. In the fall of 1863 the second quartermaster general, Alexander R. Lawton, organized a fleet of ships to outrun the Union blockade. The fleet was highly successful, and reserve stocks of clothing were in place by 1864. By then the problem was supply transportation and distribution. The result was Confederate soldiers shivering in the siege lines of Petersburg and on the march into Tennessee in late 1864 as uniforms filled warehouses in North Carolina.

Quartermaster procedures were the same on both sides. Corps, divisions, brigades, and regiments had quartermaster officers. Quartermaster officers consolidated supply requests for their unit and distributed supplies when available. After the first few months of the war arms and ammunition were plentiful for both sides.

Food for the troops

Both armies had a Subsistence Department separate from the Quartermaster Bureau. The Union army had a preexisting Subsistence Department, but it had little capacity to deal with thousands of new recruits. Lieutenant Colonel Joseph P. Taylor (brother of the former U.S. President Zachary Taylor) became commissary general of subsistence in September 1861. He set up a system in which commissary agents purchased food in major metropolitan areas. Foodstuffs were then shipped to supply depots in the field, from where unit commissary officers transported them to the troops and issued them. Beef and flour were the exceptions; armies procured them from the areas in which they operated or maintained herds of cattle on

Impressment
The seizure of private property for government use.

Commissary
A large store that sells or distributes food and other supplies to military personnel.

An illustration from Frank Leslie's Illustrated Newspaper of November 23, 1862, showing Union foraging parties returning to camp near Annandale Chapel, Virginia.

the march for fresh beef. Union soldiers were generally well fed, in addition to being plentifully supplied. On the rare occasions Union soldiers went hungry, it was because of failures in transportation or management.

Confederate shortages

Confederate commissary officers encountered genuine shortages of foodstuffs. Commissary General Lucius B. Northrop operated with a very small staff, which could not meet the needs of his demanding position. His abrasive personality made it difficult to implement reform. As the war went on, Union occupation of food-producing regions such as Tennessee worsened food shortages, as did Union control of the Mississippi River, which isolated Texas, an important food source, from the rest of the South. Inflation and the limited Confederate transportation network made food procurement difficult. Confederate soldiers rarely received the quantity or quality of rations of their Union counterparts. In 1864 Robert E. Lee told President Jefferson Davis that the food shortages were having a harmful effect. Extensive foraging by Confederate units in their own territory was inefficient, wasteful, and caused discontent among the local Southern population.

Despite the difficulties, the quartermaster and his departments on both sides did remarkably well. Civil War soldiers were generally well supplied and clothed, and usually adequately if not well fed.

Training

The huge influx of volunteers into the armies at the outbreak of the war created a challenge for the military authorities of both sides. The thousands of newly enlisted citizen-soldiers had to be transformed into well-trained units.

Many of the first volunteers joined on a wave of patriotic fervor. By summer 1861, it was obvious their enthusiasm would not be enough to obtain victory. The Union defeat at the First Battle of Bull Run (Manassas) on July 21 was a wake-up call for the North, and one experienced soldiers such as Union General William T. Sherman took to heart. The volunteers of April 1861 had to be taught how to be soldiers.

Volunteers began their training in a camp of instruction situated in the nearest large town. Here, recruits were formed into regiments and issued uniforms, weapons, and other equipment. Life in the training camp was not always comfortable. For example, at Camp Seward in New York cavalry recruits shivering in their tents were in danger of freezing to death in the bitter winter of 1861 until local residents offered to house them.

Volunteer officers

From the beginning the work of training the new recruits had its difficulties. A major problem was a lack of experienced officers who knew how to drill. Most officers were novices themselves and were learning from tactical manuals at the same time as trying to instruct their men. The situation could lead to chaos on the parade ground. One New Hampshire soldier remembered his regiment getting into a mess when the officers attempted to drill them for the first time after "cramming Casey for a fortnight." Silas Casey's *Infantry Tactics* was just one of three major drill manuals in use at the time, which added to the

Curriculum Context

Students who are describing life on campaign might mention how cold soldiers often were in the winter.

Tactical manuals

Since the 17th and 18th centuries, manuals had illustrated the individual movements soldiers used to maneuver and fire in formation on the battlefield.

confusion. The other two standard manuals were William J. Hardee's *Rifle and Light Infantry Tactics* (known as Hardee's Tactics) and General Winfield Scott's three-volume *Infantry Tactics*. As well as the official manuals, volunteers could select from a wide range of commercial instruction books that appeared once war broke out. The thousands of civilians desperate to learn how to be soldiers created a huge demand for these publications. Among the titles were Baxter's *Volunteer's Manual*, and Patten's *Infantry Tactics and Bayonet Exercise*. Patten's book sold more than 10,000 copies by the end of 1861.

Using common sense

Sometimes officers dispensed with manuals altogether and just invented commands, relying on their soldiers' common sense. Despite his earlier service in the U.S. Army, Ulysses S. Grant, like many volunteer officers, at first had trouble putting his men through drill. When the future Union general-in-chief took over his first wartime command as colonel of the 21st Illinois in June 1861, he had not drilled a unit of troops since his days at the U.S. Military Academy at West Point. He later wrote in his memoirs that he had "never looked at a copy of tactics from the time of my graduation" and, in fact, had been "near the foot of the class." Grant joked that he had to learn how to maneuver troops effectively and precisely or else clear away surrounding "houses and gardens to make room." Grant bluffed his way using the little he knew of Hardee's *Tactics*: "I found no trouble in giving commands that would

Curriculum Context

As one of the most influential commanders in the war, Ulysses S. Grant is studied in many curricula.

A Union battery at drill in Georgia. Artillerymen had to be trained to handle, maneuver, and fire field guns.

take my regiment where I wanted it to go and carry it around obstacles. I do not believe that the officers of the regiment ever discovered that I had never studied the tactics that I used."

Imposing order

By the fall of 1861 order was being imposed in the Union army, and infantry recruits could expect rigorous training for up to eight hours a day. It began with the fundamentals every soldier had to master, including marching in time and weapons drills, and moved on to tactical training, first in squads, then in companies, and later in large-scale maneuvers of battalions and brigades. The work was ceaseless. The day might begin with squad drill, followed by company drill and battalion drill in the afternoon. At the same time, there were also skirmish drills to learn and more weapons training.

Training for those of higher rank also became better organized. The senior officers of Union regiments often held night schools for their field officers and noncommissioned officers (NCOs) in which army regulations and the tactical manuals were studied.

Cavalry training

Confederate cavalry recruits were often from a rural background and proficient horsemen from the outset. However, in the Union many cavalry recruits had to be taught how to handle and take care of their horses. They learned about saddlery and harness and basic saber drill. Only then did their mounted training begin. The cavalry had an official instruction manual, Cooke's *Tactics*, which described in detail the correct posture of a mounted trooper.

Cavalry commands were issued by both voice and bugle. A cavalry recruit had to memorize 38 different bugle calls that organized his day and sent him

Skirmish
A brief fight or encounter between small groups of soldiers, rather than large armies.

Saber
A heavy cavalry sword with one sharp edge and a slightly curved blade.

Training Manuals

Officers learned how to drill their men partly through the study of instruction manuals. Before the war the most widely used manual was General Winfield Scott's *Infantry Tactics*, published in 1835. It was very technical and difficult to learn, since it had been adapted from a French manual and was written by a professional soldier for other professionals. Maneuvers could be slow and cumbersome, because each command was followed by a "halt."

Scott's *Infantry Tactics* was based on the use of the smoothbore musket, but by the end of the 1850s the introduction of the rifled musket meant that a new instruction manual was necessary. It arrived in 1860 with the publication of *Rifle and Light Infantry Tactics*, written by William J. Hardee. It was a revision of Scott's manual and described many of the infantry tactics used during the Civil War. It also took into account the longer range of the rifled musket and instructed officers how to move their men quickly over the battlefield by marching them at the "double-quick," which was a rapid rate of 180 steps per minute. At the outbreak of war Hardee's *Tactics* was the best-known military manual and was published in both the North and South. Northern editions took Hardee's name off the cover because he joined the Confederate army. Hardee's manual was replaced in 1862 by Silas Casey's *Infantry Tactics*. Casey was a Union brigadier general and used his experience of the fighting in Virginia to improve Hardee's book. Casey simplified maneuvers and drills, cut out the jargon, and instructed his readers to make their orders clear and concise. Like Hardee's manual, Casey's *Tactics* was read by both sides.

Curriculum Context

You might be asked to assess the influence of the cavalry on the overall conflict, and particularly the role of cavalry raids.

instructions in battle. The calls became second nature to both soldiers and horses. Horses pricked up their ears on hearing the "boots and saddles" signal, which indicated that it was time for the cavalryman to get himself and his horse equipped and ready. In 1863 Union cavalry tactics and training were overhauled following a lackluster performance in the first two years. From then on recruits were given even more thorough training and drilling.

Artillery

Artillerymen only received instruction in handling and firing field guns when their basic training as soldiers was complete. In the Union army the would-be gunners were able to train with gun, limber (wheeled gun carriage), caisson (ammunition chest), and a horse team. In the Confederate army, however, the shortage of artillery pieces meant that some batteries lacked equipment for months. The Surry Light Artillery of Virginia was forced to begin the war training as infantry and did not receive any cannons until September 1861. Even then they had to maneuver their guns manually because they had no horse teams. It was not until December that enough horses arrived for the battery to train properly.

Armies in the field

While on active campaign, troops rarely had time for further training, although most commanders put their regiments through drill practice before the start of the spring campaigning season. This served to get the men fit after the long months spent idle in winter camp.

As the war went on and the soldiers grew in experience, the training of new recruits sometimes took place with the army in the field rather than in a training camp. The newcomers arrived untrained at their units to be instructed by veteran NCOs. While this suited the veterans, for the recruits it could be a hard introduction to army life as the impatience of the veterans often made the process a miserable one. In a letter of 1862 a Massachusetts recruit complained the men training him were sick of soldiering and had "no ambition to teach others."

Battery
A group of artillery guns such as cannons or mortars, with their supporting equipment, horses, and gun crews.

NCOs
Noncommissioned officers: junior officers who have been promoted from within the ranks.

A sketch by Alfred Waud showing Union sailors practicing fighting with swords.

Uniforms

In 1861 soldiers went to war dressed in a wide variety of uniforms. On both sides ranks were filled with companies and regiments of city and state militia that had highly individualistic ideas of what a soldier should look like.

Some regiments of first- or second-generation Americans copied the uniforms of their home countries. The 79th New York State Militia looked to its Scottish ancestry, adopting trews (trousers) made of the Cameron clan tartan and the Scottish Glengarry cap. In full dress the 79th even wore kilts, though never in battle. Another Union regiment, the 39th New York, known as the Garibaldi Guard, was made up of Italian Americans who copied the uniforms of the famous Italian light infantry, the Bersaglieri. They wore red shirts and distinctive broad-brimmed hats trimmed with cock feathers.

France had the biggest foreign influence on Civil War uniforms. The French Zouave uniforms, inspired by North African dress, were copied by regiments in both the North and South, while early in the war the Union army quartermaster considered dressing all U.S. infantry like French chasseurs (infantry), with short blue jackets and baggy yellow pants clasped by gaiters.

Inspiration from the past

The Putnam Phalanx company of Connecticut copied the dress of George Washington's troops of the 1780s and wore tricorne hats and swallow tailcoats. The tailcoat also proved popular with the other units, recalling as it did the great military age of Napoleon in the early 1800s. One reason for these ornate uniforms was a belief that a soldier should look dashing and colorful, and that men would want to become soldiers so that they could wear an attractive uniform.

Zouave

An Algerian member of a French colonial regiment, distinguished by colorful uniforms.

Curriculum Context

It night be interesting to compare romantic views of soldiering before the war with the reality discovered by both soldiers and the public on both sides.

As late as 1863 the 3rd New Jersey Cavalry adopted a uniform copied from the Austrian light cavalry. They wore a small, round pillbox hat, a jacket covered in double rows of yellow cord, and a short cape secured over one shoulder. Mocked as being fit only for the parade ground, they became known as "The Butterflies."

Blue and gray

Several Union regiments began the war wearing gray. All over the country it had been a popular color for militia units before the war; but after confusion at the First Battle of Bull Run in July 1861, when gray-clad Northerners were shot at by their fellow Unionists, regiments wearing gray changed to dark blue. The Confederate army had a similar problem when the Maryland Guard Zouaves began fighting in 1861 wearing dark blue. Under wartime conditions uniforms became simpler and plainer, as soldiers came to realize that fancy uniforms were impractical on campaign, and both governments tried to make uniforms as cheaply as possible.

Curriculum Context

It was not unusual in the 18th and 19th centuries for armies to wear very similar uniforms, frequently causing confusion in battle.

Union infantry

According to official regulations, a Union infantryman of 1861 was meant to wear a dark-blue frock coat with a stand-up collar, dark-blue trousers, and a Hardee hat. Some Union regiments went to war wearing this, but by the end of 1861 the uniform was beginning to change as the clothing was adapted. Dark-blue trousers were replaced by light-blue because light-blue wool was cheaper. The frock coat was found to be too long for active service and was replaced by the sack coat. It was a short, loose-fitting jacket with a soft, fold-down collar secured by four large buttons. They were stamped with either the U.S. emblem or the seal of the state the regiment came from. State seals were also found on belt buckles.

Hardee hat

A felt hat that was the standard wear for Union soldiers.

The formal uniform of a Union infantryman was a mid-length dark-blue frock coat with a stand-up collar, light-blue trousers, and a broad-brimmed Hardee hat of black felt. The hat was worn with one side folded up and decorated with regimental insignia. On active service fatigues (above right) were more usual: a short, loose jacket with fold-down collar and forage cap.

The unpopular Hardee hat was often battered into a more comfortable shape. Many soldiers preferred the forage cap, a soft, peaked cap with the round top worn forward. As well as the regular type, there were two other styles of forage cap. The McDowell cap was worn with a high crown, while the McClellan cap imitated the French kepi and was usually red and highly decorated with braiding. Forage caps could be worn with waterproof oilcloth covers to keep them dry. Overcoats or greatcoats were light blue and had fitted capes. Union uniforms were made in a thick, coarse woolen cloth called kersey. There was no light uniform issued for summer, and the Union troops just had to suffer in the heat. Many soldiers solved the problem by wearing looted items of Confederate uniform, which were often made of cotton or denim.

Confederate infantry

The style of Confederate infantry uniforms was set down in regulations of June 1861. They established gray as the uniform color. The trousers were to be light blue and the tunic was to be hip-length. Since the Confederate government had no money to supply uniforms, it had to rely on state governments to clothe their own regiments. Most kept to the regulations, but there were some interesting variations from state to state. Some South Carolina regiments wore long pleated hunting jackets, while troops from the warmer climate of the Deep South dispensed with jackets altogether and just wore fatigue shirts trimmed with dark blue.

By 1862 the long uniform tunic had been replaced in most regiments by a short jacket with a soft stand-up collar fastened by nine buttons usually stamped with the seal or crest of the regiment's home state. Like the state regiments of the North, state seals were also stamped on belt buckles.

Many colors

The color of the Confederate uniforms varied widely as the war went on. The South had to rely on vegetable dyes to try to produce gray, but most attempts bleached under the sun and turned a light brown color. Because of this Southern troops were sometimes referred to as "butternuts."

Curriculum Context

Fashion historians often argue that bright colors disappeared from the battlefield because they made soldiers too obvious as targets for gunpowder weapons.

Butternut

A light brown dye produced by the bark of the butternut tree.

Glossary

amnesty An act by which an authority such as a government pardons a large group of individuals.

anesthesia A drug that acts as a pain killer by deadening the senses or inducing temporary unconsciousness.

arsenal A store of weapons and ammunition.

bacteria Tiny microscopic animals that transmit disease.

ballad A long song that tells a narrative, which is often melancholy or concerned with loss.

battery An artillery unit, consisting of a number of guns and their crews.

calomel Mercury chloride, used as a disinfectant and a laxative.

canton The vocabulary used to describe flag corners in heraldry.

chaplain A clergyman attached to part of the military.

classified Declared an official secret by the government.

commandeer To seize private goods for military purposes.

commerce raider A fast Confederate ship used to intercept Union merchant ships at sea and seize their cargoes.

commissary A large store that sells or distributes food and other supplies to military personnel.

compensated emancipation An alternative to the abolition of slavery under which slaveowners would be paid for the slaves they released.

cotton running Smuggling cotton out of the South through the Union blockade or over the border to Mexico.

desensitization The process of becoming immune to distress caused by witnessing terrible injuries, pain, or death.

desert To abandon one's military service without permission.

diplomatic Concerning relations and negotiations between different countries.

drill Drill was a highly repetitive series of marching exercises used by armies to ensure that soldiers learned to maneuver on the battlefield almost by instinct.

embark To go on board a ship, train, or airplane to make a journey.

equestrian statue A statue that portrays its subject on horseback.

etching A method of printing by engraving lines in a metal plate, which is then inked to produce an image on a piece of paper.

expenses The costs of living while working, such as the price of meals, lodging, and transportation.

fife A small, high-pitched flute similar to a piccolo, most often used in marching bands.

forage Food for animals.

freedmen Slaves who had been emancipated during the war.

fugitive Someone who has escaped from captivity, such as a runaway slave.

furlough An extended period of leave from duty for a soldier or other serviceman, for example to allow them to return home.

gangrene A condition when damaged tissue dies and decays, usually because of lack of blood.

garrisons Units of soldiers maintained in towns or forts in case they are required to keep order.

guerrilla A soldier who fights by ambush, raids, and sabotage, rather than regular pitched battles.

hardtack A staple food of the Civil War, hardtack was a hard biscuit made only of flour and water.

honorably discharged Having completed one's military service with a record of honest and faithful conduct.

house arrest A form of imprisonment in which the inmate lives at home but is under guard and is prevented from leaving the house or yard.

humanities Non-science subjects such as history or classics.

idyllic A view that depicts rural life as peaceful and contented.

impressment The compulsory seizure of goods by governments for public use.

infiltrate To use disguise to pass through enemy lines.

itinerant Someone who moves around, with no fixed base.

Jew's harp A small musical instrument with a protruding metal tongue; the pyre-shaped instrument is held in the mouth by one hand and the metal tongue is plucked by the other hand.

latrines Communal toilets in a barracks or camp.

lynch To put someone to death by the action of a mob, often by hanging, without legal authority.

martial law Law administered by the military services.

morale The positive quality that makes men willing to perform difficult tasks such as fighting, even in the face of huge odds.

muster To gather soldiers together in an assembly.

NCOs Noncommissioned officers; junior officers who have been promoted from within the ranks.

parole To release a prisoner on a promise that he or she will not repeat his or her offense.

periodicals A publication such as a magazine that is published regularly but with a set interval between each issue.

quinine A drug made from tree bark that helps prevent and treat malaria.

quota A required number of soldiers from each state.

reconciliation To restore former enemies to a state of friendship, for example by agreeing to disagree over their differences.

recuperation Recovering one's former health, usually through an extended period of rest.

saber A heavy cavalry sword with one sharp edge and a slightly curved blade.

shebang A word that usually describes the whole of something, as in the phrase "the whole shebang."

segregation The separation of people based on their skin color or another quality.

skirmish A brief fight or encounter between small groups of soldiers, rather than large armies.

stocisim An ability to remain indifferent to suffering and pain.

speculators Businessmen who invest in commodities in the hopes that shortages or other circumstances will allow them to make big profits in the future.

standard A long, tapering flag that belongs to an individual or organization; standards were carried on long poles to act as rallying points on the battlefield.

triage The process of sorting the wounded for priority of care: those whose lives could not be saved, those who needed immediate treatment, and those whose treatment was not so urgent.

typhoid A serious intestinal infection spread by bacteria in infected food or water.

woodblock A form of printing that carves lines into a piece of wood to print.

Zouave An Algerian member of a French colonial regiment, distinguished by colorful uniforms.

Further Research

BOOKS

Barney, William L. *The Oxford Encyclopedia of the Civil War*. Oxford University Press, 2011.

Catton, Bruce. *The Civil War*. Boston, MA: Houghton Mifflin, 1987.

Civil War Preservation Trust. *Civil War Sites: The Official Guide to the Civil War Discovery Trail*. Globe Pequot, 2007.

Coles, David J., et al. *Encyclopedia of the American Civil War: Political, Social, and Military History*. W.W. Norton and Company, 2002.

Cornelius, Steven H. *Music of the Civil War Era*. Greenwood, 2004.

Goldfield, David. *America Aflame: How the Civil War Created a Nation*. Bloomsbury Press, 2011.

Gragg, Rod. *From Fields of Fire and Glory: Letters of the Civil War*. Chronicle Books, 2002.

Harper, Judith E. *Women During the Civil War: An Encyclopedia*. Routledge, 2007.

Hendrickson, Robert. *The Road to Appomattox*. New York: John Wiley, 1998.

Holzer, Harold, and Craig Symonds. *The New York Times Complete Civil War 1861–1865*. Black Dog and Leventhal Publishers, 2010.

Kelbaugh, Ross J. *Introduction to Civil War Photography*. Gettysburg, PA: Thomas Publications, 1991.

McPherson, James M. *Battle Cry of Freedom*. New York: Oxford University Press, 1988.

Manning, Chandra. *What This Cruel War Was Over: Soldiers, Slavery, and the Civil War*. Vintage, 2008.

Markle, Donald E. *Spies and Spymasters of the Civil War*. Hippocrene Books, 2004.

Rable, George C. *God's Almost Chosen Peoples: A Religious History of the American Civil War*. University of North Carolina Press, 2010.

Roberts, William H. *Civil War Ironclads: The U.S. Navy and Industrial Mobilization*. The Johns Hopkins University Press, 2007.

Robertson, James I. *Soldiers Blue and Gray*. Columbia, SC: University of South Carolina Press, 1998.

Ross, Charles D. *Trial By Fire: Science, Technology, and the Civil War*. White Mane Publishing Company, 2000.

Schecter, Barnet. *The Devil's Own Work: The Civil War Draft Riots and the Fight to Reconstruct America*. Walker & Company, 2007.

Schroeder-Lein, Glenna R. *The Encyclopedia of Civil War Medicine*. M.E. Sharpe, 2008.

Stern, Philip Van Doren. *Soldier Life in the Union and Confederate Armies*. Gramercy, 2001.

Taylor, Amy Murrell. *The Divided Family in Civil War America*. University of North Carolina Press, 2009.

Trudeau, Noah. *Like Men of War: Black Troops in the Civil War, 1862–1865*. New York: Little, Brown, and Co, 1998.

Varhola, Michael J. *Life in Civil War America*. Family Tree Books, 2011.

Wiley, Bell Irvin. *The Life of Johnny Reb: The Common Soldier of the Confederacy*. Baton Rouge, LA: Louisiana State University Press, 1980.

Wiley, Bell Irvin. *The Life of Billy Yank: The Common Soldier of the Union*. Baton Rouge, LA: Louisiana State University Press, 1981.

Woodworth, Steven E. *American Civil War* (Gale Library of Daily Life). Gale, 2008.

Wright, Mark. *What They Didn't Teach You about the Civil War*. Novato, CA: Presidio Press, 1996.

Zeller, Bob. *The Blue and Gray in Black and White: A History of Civil War Photography*. Praeger, 2005.

INTERNET RESOURCES

These general sites have comprehensive links to a large number of Civil War topics:

http://sunsite.utk.edu/civil-war/warweb.html

http://civilwarhome.com/

http://americancivilwar.com/

http://www.civil-war.net/

http://www2.cr.nps.gov/abpp/battles/bystate.htm
This part of the National Parks Service site allows you to search for battles by state

http://pdmusic.org/civilwar.html
Sound files and words to Civil War songs

http://www.civilwarmed.org/
National Museum of Civil War Medicine

http://memory.loc.gov/ammem/aaohtml/exhibit/aopart4.html
Civil War section of the African American Odyssey online exhibition at the Library of Congress

http://valley.vcdh.virginia.edu/
The Valley of the Shadow Project: details of Civil War life in two communities, one Northern and one Southern

http://www.civilwarhome.com/records.htm
Battle reports by commanding generals from the Official Records

http://www.cwc.lsu.edu/
The United States Civil War Center at Lousiana State University

http://www.nps.gov/gett/gettkidz/soldslang.htm
Civil War slang from the site of the Gettysburg National Military Park

http://www.sonofthesouth.net/leefoundation/ebooks.htm
The Robert E. Lee Foundation digital library of books about Lee and about the Civil War generally

Index

Page numbers in *italic* refer to illustrations and captions.